Department of the Treasury
Internal Revenue Service

Publication 15
Cat. No. 10000W

(Circular E), Employer's Tax Guide

For use in **2016**

Get forms and other information faster and easier at:
- *IRS.gov* (English)
- *IRS.gov/Korean* (한국어)
- *IRS.gov/Spanish* (Español)
- *IRS.gov/Russian* (Русский)
- *IRS.gov/Chinese* (   )
- *IRS.gov/Vietnamese* (TiếngViệt)

Dec 23, 2015

Contents

Future Developments

For the latest information about developments related to Pub. 15, such as legislation enacted after it was published, go to *www.irs.gov/pub15*.

What's New

Social security and Medicare tax for 2016. The social security tax rate is 6.2% each for the employee and employer, unchanged from 2015. The social security wage base limit is $118,500, unchanged from 2015.

The Medicare tax rate is 1.45% each for the employee and employer, unchanged from 2015. There is no wage base limit for Medicare tax.

Social security and Medicare taxes apply to the wages of household workers you pay $2,000 or more in cash or an equivalent form of compensation. Social security and Medicare taxes apply to election workers who are paid $1,700 or more in cash or an equivalent form of compensation.

2016 withholdng tables. This publication includes the 2016 Percentage Method Tables and Wage Bracket Tables for Income Tax Withholding.

Withholding allowance. The 2016 amount for one withholding allowance on an annual basis is $4,050.

New filing due date for 2016 Forms W-2, W-3, and 1099-MISC. Both paper and electronically filed 2016 Forms W-2 and W-3 must be filed with the Social Security Administration (SSA) by January 31, 2017. Both paper and electronically filed 2016 Form 1099-MISC must be filed with the IRS by January 31, 2017.

Work opportunity tax credit for qualified tax-exempt organizations hiring qualified veterans extended. The work opportunity tax credit is now available for eligible unemployed veterans who begin work after December 31, 2014, and before January 1, 2020. Qualified tax-exempt organizations that hire eligible unemployed veterans can claim the work opportunity tax credit against their payroll tax liability using Form 5884-C. For more information, visit IRS.gov and enter "work opportunity tax credit" in the search box.

New Pub. 5146 explains employment tax examinations and appeal rights. Pub. 5146 provides employers with information on how the IRS selects employment tax returns to be examined, what happens during an exam, and what options an employer has in responding to the results of an exam, including how to appeal the results. Pub. 5146 also includes information on worker classification issues and tip exams.

Motion picture project employers. Beginning January 1, 2016, all wages paid by a motion picture project employer to a motion picture project worker during a calendar year are subject to a single social security tax wage base ($118,500 for 2016) and a single FUTA tax wage base ($7,000 for 2016) regardless of the worker's status as a common law employee of multiple clients of the motion picture project employer. For more information, including the definition of a motion picture project employer and motion picture project worker, see Internal Revenue Code section 3512.

Reminders

COBRA premium assistance credit. Effective for tax periods beginning after December 31, 2013, the credit for COBRA premium assistance payments can't be claimed on Form 941, Employer's QUARTERLY Federal Tax Return (or Form 944, Employer's ANNUAL Federal Tax Return). Instead, after filing your Form 941 (or Form 944), file Form 941-X, Adjusted Employer's QUARTERLY Federal Tax Return or Claim for Refund (or Form 944-X, Adjusted Employer's ANNUAL Federal Tax Return or Claim for Refund), respectively, to claim the COBRA premium assistance credit. Filing a Form 941-X (or Form 944-X) before filing a Form 941 (or Form 944) for the return period may result in errors or delays in processing your Form 941-X (or Form 944-X). For more information, see the Instructions for Form 941 (or the Instructions for Form 944), or visit IRS.gov and enter "COBRA" in the search box.

Medicaid waiver payments. Notice 2014-7 provides that certain Medicaid waiver payments are excludable from income for federal income tax purposes. See Notice 2014-7, 2014-4 I.R.B. 445, available at *www.irs.gov/irb/ 2014-4_IRB/ar06.html*. For more information, including questions and answers related to Notice 2014-7, visit IRS.gov and enter "Medicaid waiver payments" in the search box.

No federal income tax withholding on disability payments for injuries incurred as a direct result of a terrorist attack directed against the United States. Disability payments for injuries incurred as a direct result of a terrorist attack directed against the United States (or its allies) aren't included in income. Because federal income tax withholding is only required when a payment is includable in income, no federal income tax should be withheld from these payments.

Voluntary withholding on dividends and other distributions by an Alaska Native Corporation (ANC). A shareholder of an ANC may request voluntary income tax withholding on dividends and other distributions paid by an ANC. A shareholder may request voluntary withholding by giving the ANC a completed Form W-4V. For more information see Notice 2013-77, 2013-50 I.R.B. 632, available at *www.irs.gov/irb/2013-50_IRB/ar10.html*.

Same-sex marriage. For federal tax purposes, marriages of couples of the same sex are treated the same as marriages of couples of the opposite sex. The term "spouse" includes an individual married to a person of the same sex. However, individuals who have entered into a registered domestic partnership, civil union, or other similar relationship that isn't considered a marriage under state law aren't considered married for federal tax purposes. For more information, see Revenue Ruling 2013-17, 2013-38 I.R.B. 201, available at *www.irs.gov/irb/ 2013-38_IRB/ar07.html* .

Notice 2013-61 provides special administrative procedures for employers to make claims for refunds or adjustments of overpayments of social security and Medicare taxes with respect to certain same-sex spouse benefits before expiration of the period of limitations. Notice 2013-61, 2013-44 I.R.B. 432, is available at *www.irs.gov/ irb/2013-44_IRB/ar10.html*. You may correct errors to federal income tax withholding and Additional Medicare Tax withheld for prior years if the amount reported on your employment tax return doesn't agree with the amount you actually withheld. This type of error is an administrative error. You may also correct errors to federal income tax withholding and Additional Medicare Tax withheld for prior years if section 3509 rates apply.

Additional Medicare Tax withholding. In addition to withholding Medicare tax at 1.45%, you must withhold a 0.9% Additional Medicare Tax from wages you pay to an employee in excess of $200,000 in a calendar year. You are required to begin withholding Additional Medicare Tax in the pay period in which you pay wages in excess of $200,000 to an employee and continue to withhold it each pay period until the end of the calendar year. Additional Medicare Tax is only imposed on the employee. There is no employer share of Additional Medicare Tax. All wages that are subject to Medicare tax are subject to Additional Medicare Tax withholding if paid in excess of the $200,000 withholding threshold.

For more information on what wages are subject to Medicare tax, see the chart, *Special Rules for Various Types of Services and Payments*, in section 15. For more information on Additional Medicare Tax, visit IRS.gov and enter "Additional Medicare Tax" in the search box.

Outsourcing payroll duties. You are responsible to ensure that tax returns are filed and deposits and payments are made, even if you contract with a third party to perform these acts. You remain responsible if the third party fails to perform any required action. If you choose to outsource any of your payroll and related tax duties (that is, withholding, reporting, and paying over social security, Medicare, FUTA, and income taxes) to a third-party payer, such as a payroll service provider (PSP) or reporting agent, visit IRS.gov and enter "outsourcing payroll duties" in the search box for helpful information on this topic. For more information on the different types of third party payer arrangements, see section 16.

Severance payments are subject to social security and Medicare taxes, income tax withholding, and FUTA tax. Severance payments are wages subject to social security and Medicare taxes. As noted in section 15, *Special Rules for Various Types of Services and Payments*, severance payments are also subject to income tax withholding and FUTA tax.

You must receive written notice from the IRS to file Form 944. If you have been filing Forms 941 (or Forms 941-SS, Employer's QUARTERLY Federal Tax Return—American Samoa, Guam, the Commonwealth of the Northern Mariana Islands, and the U.S. Virgin Islands, or Formularios 941-PR, Planilla para la Declaración Federal TRIMESTRAL del Patrono), and believe your employment taxes for the calendar year will be $1,000 or less, and you would like to file Form 944 instead of Forms 941, you must contact the IRS to request to file Form 944. You must receive written notice from the IRS to file Form 944 instead of Forms 941 before you may file this form. For more information on requesting to file Form 944, see the Instructions for Form 944.

Employers can request to file Forms 941 instead of Form 944. If you received notice from the IRS to file Form 944 but would like to file Forms 941 instead, you must contact the IRS to request to file Forms 941. You must receive written notice from the IRS to file Forms 941 instead of Form 944 before you may file these forms. For more information on requesting to file Form 941, see the Instructions for Form 944.

Federal tax deposits must be made by electronic funds transfer (EFT). You must use EFT to make all federal tax deposits. Generally, an EFT is made using the Electronic Federal Tax Payment System (EFTPS). If you don't want to use EFTPS, you can arrange for your tax professional, financial institution, payroll service, or other trusted third party to make electronic deposits on your behalf. Also, you may arrange for your financial institution to initiate a same-day wire payment on your behalf. EFTPS is a free service provided by the Department of Treasury. Services provided by your tax professional, financial institution, payroll service, or other third party may have a fee.

For more information on making federal tax deposits, see *How To Deposit* in section 11. To get more information about EFTPS or to enroll in EFTPS, visit *www.eftps.gov*, or call 1-800-555-4477 or 1-800-733-4829 (TDD). Additional information about EFTPS is also available in Pub. 966.

Aggregate Form 941 filers. Agents must complete Schedule R (Form 941), Allocation Schedule for Aggregate Form 941 Filers, when filing an aggregate Form 941. Aggregate Forms 941 may only be filed by agents approved by the IRS under section 3504 of the Internal Revenue Code (IRC). To request approval to act as an agent for an employer, the agent files Form 2678 with the IRS.

Aggregate Form 940 filers. Agents must complete Schedule R (Form 940), Allocation Schedule for Aggregate Form 940 Filers, when filing an aggregate Form 940, Employer's Annual Federal Unemployment (FUTA) Tax Return. Aggregate Forms 940 can be filed by agents acting on behalf of home care service recipients who receive home care services through a program administered by a federal, state, or local government. To request approval to act as an agent on behalf of home care service recipients, the agent files Form 2678 with the IRS.

Electronic Filing and Payment

Now, more than ever before, businesses can enjoy the benefits of filing and paying their federal taxes electronically. Whether you rely on a tax professional or handle your own taxes, the IRS offers you convenient programs to make filing and payment easier.

Spend less time and worry on taxes and more time running your business. Use *e-file* and EFTPS to your benefit.

- For *e-file,* visit *www.irs.gov/efile* for additional information.

- For EFTPS, visit *www.eftps.gov* or call EFTPS Customer Service at 1-800-555-4477 or 1-800-733-4829 (TDD).

- For electronic filing of Forms W-2, Wage and Tax Statement, visit *www.socialsecurity.gov/employer*.

 If you are filing your tax return or paying your federal taxes electronically, a valid EIN is required. If a valid EIN isn't provided, the return or payment won't be processed. This may result in penalties and delays in processing your return or payment.

Electronic funds withdrawal (EFW). If you file Form 940, Form 941, Form 944, or Form 945 electronically, you can e-file and e-pay (electronic funds withdrawal) the balance due in a single step using tax preparation software or through a tax professional. However, don't use EFW to make federal tax deposits. For more information on paying your taxes using EFW, visit the IRS website at *www.irs.gov/payments*. A fee may be charged to file electronically.

Credit or debit card payments. For information on paying your taxes with a credit or debit card, visit the IRS website at *www.irs.gov/payments*. However, don't use credit or debit cards to make federal tax deposits.

Online payment agreement. You may be eligible to apply for an installment agreement online if you have a balance due when you file your employment tax return. For more information, see the instructions for your employment tax return or visit the IRS website at *www.irs.gov/payments*.

Forms in Spanish

You can provide Formulario W-4(SP), Certificado de Exención de Retenciones del Empleado, in place of Form W-4, Employee's Withholding Allowance Certificate, to your Spanish-speaking employees. For more information, see Pub. 17(SP), El Impuesto Federal sobre los Ingresos (Para Personas Físicas). For nonemployees, Formulario W-9(SP), Solicitud y Certificación del Número de Identificación del Contribuyente, may be used in place of Form W-9, Request for Taxpayer Identification Number and Certification.

Hiring New Employees

Eligibility for employment. You must verify that each new employee is legally eligible to work in the United States. This includes completing the U.S. Citizenship and Immigration Services (USCIS) Form I-9, Employment Eligibility Verification. You can get Form I-9 from USCIS offices or by calling 1-800-870-3676. For more information, visit the USCIS website at *www.uscis.gov*, or call 1-800-375-5283 or 1-800-767-1833 (TDD).

New hire reporting. You are required to report any new employee to a designated state new hire registry. A new employee is an employee who hasn't previously been employed by you or was previously employed by you but has been separated from such prior employment for at least 60 consecutive days.

Many states accept a copy of Form W-4 with employer information added. Visit the Office of Child Support Enforcement website at *www.acf.hhs.gov/programs/cse/newhire* for more information.

W-4 request. Ask each new employee to complete the 2016 Form W-4. See section 9.

Name and social security number (SSN). Record each new employee's name and SSN from his or her social security card. Any employee without a social security card should apply for one. See section 4.

Paying Wages, Pensions, or Annuities

Correcting Form 941 or Form 944. If you discover an error on a previously filed Form 941 or Form 944, make the correction using Form 941-X or Form 944-X. Forms 941-X and 944-X are stand-alone forms, meaning taxpayers can file them when an error is discovered. Forms 941-X and 944-X are used by employers to claim refunds or abatements of employment taxes, rather than Form 843. See section 13 for more information.

Income tax withholding. Withhold federal income tax from each wage payment or supplemental unemployment compensation plan benefit payment according to the employee's Form W-4 and the correct withholding table. If you have nonresident alien employees, see *Withholding income taxes on the wages of nonresident alien employees* in section 9.

Withhold from periodic **pension and annuity payments** as if the recipient is married claiming three withholding allowances, unless he or she has provided Form W-4P, Withholding Certificate for Pension or Annuity Payments, either electing no withholding or giving a different number of allowances, marital status, or an additional amount to be withheld. Don't withhold on direct rollovers from qualified plans or governmental section 457(b) plans. See section 9 and Pub. 15-A, Employer's Supplemental Tax Guide. Pub. 15-A includes information about withholding on pensions and annuities.

Zero wage return. If you haven't filed a "final" Form 941 or Form 944, or aren't a "seasonal" employer, you must continue to file a Form 941 or Form 944, even for periods during which you paid no wages. The IRS encourages you to file your "Zero Wage" Forms 941 or 944 electronically using IRS e-file at *www.irs.gov/efile*.

Information Returns

You may be required to file information returns to report certain types of payments made during the year. For example, you must file Form 1099-MISC, Miscellaneous Income, to report payments of $600 or more to persons not treated as employees (for example, independent contractors) for services performed for your trade or business. For details about filing Forms 1099 and for information about required electronic filing, see the General Instructions for Certain Information Returns for general information and the separate, specific instructions for each information return you file (for example, Instructions for Form 1099-MISC). Generally, don't use Forms 1099 to report wages and other compensation you paid to employees; report these on Form W-2. See the General Instructions for Forms W-2 and W-3 for details about filing Form W-2 and for information about required electronic filing. If you file 250 or more Forms 1099, you must file them electronically. If you file 250 or more Forms W-2, you must file them electronically. IRS and SSA won't accept information returns filed on magnetic media.

Information reporting customer service site. The IRS operates an information return customer service site to answer questions about reporting on Forms W-2, W-3, 1099, and other information returns. If you have questions related to reporting on information returns, call 1-866-455-7438 (toll free), 304-263-8700 (toll call), or 304-579-4827 (TDD/TTY for persons who are deaf, hard of hearing, or have a speech disability). The center can also be reached by email at *mccirp@irs.gov*. Don't include tax identification numbers (TINs) or attachments in email correspondence because electronic mail isn't secure.

Nonpayroll Income Tax Withholding

Nonpayroll federal income tax withholding (reported on Forms 1099 and Form W-2G, Certain Gambling Winnings) must be reported on Form 945, Annual Return of Withheld Federal Income Tax. Separate deposits are required for payroll (Form 941 or Form 944) and nonpayroll (Form 945) withholding. Nonpayroll items include:

- Pensions (including distributions from tax-favored retirement plans, for example, section 401(k), section 403(b), and governmental section 457(b) plans) and annuities.

- Military retirement.

- Gambling winnings.

- Indian gaming profits.

- Certain other payments, such as unemployment compensation, social security, and Tier 1 railroad retirement benefits, subject to voluntary withholding.

- Payments subject to backup withholding.

For details on depositing and reporting nonpayroll income tax withholding, see the Instructions for Form 945.

Distributions from nonqualified pension plans and deferred compensation plans. Because distributions to participants from some nonqualified pension plans and deferred compensation plans (including section 457(b) plans of tax-exempt organizations) are treated as wages and are reported on Form W-2, income tax withheld must be reported on Form 941 or Form 944, not on Form 945. However, distributions from such plans to a beneficiary or estate of a deceased employee aren't wages and are reported on Forms 1099-R, Distributions From Pensions,

Employer Responsibilities

Employer Responsibilities: The following list provides a brief summary of your basic responsibilities. Because the individual circumstances for each employer can vary greatly, responsibilities for withholding, depositing, and reporting employment taxes can differ. Each item in this list has a page reference to a more detailed discussion in this publication.

New Employees:	Page
☐ Verify work eligibility of new employees	4
☐ Record employees' names and SSNs from social security cards	4
☐ Ask employees for Form W-4	4
Each Payday:	
☐ Withhold federal income tax based on each employee's Form W-4	20
☐ Withhold employee's share of social security and Medicare taxes	23
☐ Deposit:	
• Withheld income tax	
• Withheld and employer social security taxes	
• Withheld and employer Medicare taxes	24
Note: *Due date of deposit generally depends on your deposit schedule (monthly or semiweekly)*	
Quarterly (By April 30, July 31, October 31, and January 31):	
☐ Deposit FUTA tax if undeposited amount is over $500	35
☐ File Form 941 (pay tax with return if not required to deposit)	29

Annually (By January 31 of the current year, for the prior year):	Page
☐ File Form 944 if required (pay tax with return if not required to deposit)	29
Annually (see *Calendar* for due dates):	
☐ Remind employees to submit a new Form W-4 if they need to change their withholding	20
☐ Ask for a new Form W-4 from employees claiming exemption from income tax withholding	20
☐ Reconcile Forms 941 (or Form 944) with Forms W-2 and W-3	31
☐ Furnish each employee a Form W-2	7
☐ File Copy A of Forms W-2 and the transmittal Form W-3 with the SSA	8
☐ Furnish each other payee a Form 1099 (for example, Form 1099-MISC)	7
☐ File Forms 1099 and the transmittal Form 1096	8
☐ File Form 940	7
☐ File Form 945 for any nonpayroll income tax withholding	8

Annuities, Retirement or Profit-Sharing Plans, IRAs, Insurance Contracts, etc.; income tax withheld must be reported on Form 945.

Backup withholding. You generally must withhold 28% of certain taxable payments if the payee fails to furnish you with his or her correct taxpayer identification number (TIN). This withholding is referred to as "backup withholding."

Payments subject to backup withholding include interest, dividends, patronage dividends, rents, royalties, commissions, nonemployee compensation, payments made in settlement of payment card or third-party network transactions, and certain other payments you make in the course of your trade or business. In addition, transactions by brokers and barter exchanges and certain payments made by fishing boat operators are subject to backup withholding.

 Backup withholding doesn't apply to wages, pensions, annuities, IRAs (including simplified employee pension (SEP) and SIMPLE retirement plans), section 404(k) distributions from an employee stock ownership plan (ESOP), medical savings accounts (MSAs), health savings accounts (HSAs), long-term-care benefits, or real estate transactions.

You can use Form W-9 or Formulario W-9(SP) to request payees to furnish a TIN. Form W-9 or Formulario W-9 (SP) must be used when payees must certify that the number furnished is correct, or when payees must certify that they aren't subject to backup withholding or are exempt from backup withholding. The Instructions for the Requester of Form W-9 or Formulario W-9(SP) includes a list of types of payees who are exempt from backup withholding. For more information, see Pub. 1281, Backup Withholding for Missing and Incorrect Name/TIN(s).

Recordkeeping

Keep all records of employment taxes for at least 4 years. These should be available for IRS review. Your records should include the following information.

- Your EIN.

- Amounts and dates of all wage, annuity, and pension payments.

- Amounts of tips reported to you by your employees.

- Records of allocated tips.

- The fair market value of in-kind wages paid.

- Names, addresses, social security numbers, and occupations of employees and recipients.

- Any employee copies of Forms W-2 and W-2c returned to you as undeliverable.

- Dates of employment for each employee.

- Periods for which employees and recipients were paid while absent due to sickness or injury and the amount

and weekly rate of payments you or third party payors made to them.

- Copies of employees' and recipients' income tax withholding allowance certificates (Forms W-4, W-4P, W-4(SP), W-4S, and W-4V).

- Dates and amounts of tax deposits you made and acknowledgment numbers for deposits made by EFTPS.

- Copies of returns filed and confirmation numbers.

- Records of fringe benefits and expense reimbursements provided to your employees, including substantiation.

Change of Business Name

Notify the IRS immediately if you change your business name. Write to the IRS office where you file your returns, using the *Without a payment* address provided in the instructions for your employment tax return, to notify the IRS of any business name change. See Pub. 1635 to see if you need to apply for a new EIN.

Change of Business Address or Responsible Party

Notify the IRS immediately if you change your business address or responsible party. Complete and mail Form 8822-B to notify the IRS of a business address or responsible party change. For a definition of "responsible party," see the Form 8822-B instructions.

Private Delivery Services

You can use certain private delivery services designated by the IRS to mail tax returns and payments. The list includes only the following:

- Federal Express (FedEx): FedEx First Overnight, FedEx Priority Overnight, FedEx Standard Overnight, FedEx 2 Day, FedEx International Next Flight Out, FedEx International Priority, FedEx International First, and FedEx International Economy

- United Parcel Service (UPS): UPS Next Day Air Early AM, UPS Next Day Air, UPS Next Day Air Saver, UPS 2nd Day Air, UPS 2nd Day Air A.M., UPS Worldwide Express Plus, and UPS Worldwide Express

For the IRS mailing address to use if you are using a private delivery service, go to IRS.gov and enter "private delivery service" in the search box.

Your private delivery service can tell you how to get written proof of the mailing date.

Private delivery services can't deliver items to P.O. boxes. You must use the U.S. Postal Service to mail any item to an IRS P.O. box address.

Telephone Help

Tax questions. You can call the IRS Business and Specialty Tax Line with your employment tax questions at 1-800-829-4933.

Help for people with disabilities. You may call 1-800-829-4059 (TDD/TTY for persons who are deaf, hard of hearing, or have a speech disability) with any employment tax questions. You may also use this number for assistance with unresolved tax problems.

Additional employment tax information. Visit IRS.gov and enter "employment taxes" in the search box.

Ordering Employer Tax Forms and Publications

You can order employer tax forms and publications and information returns online at *www.irs.gov/orderforms*.

Instead of ordering paper Forms W-2 and W-3, consider filing them electronically using the SSA's free e-file service. Visit the SSA's Employer W-2 Filing Instructions & Information website at *www.socialsecurity.gov/employer* to register for Business Services Online. You will be able to create Forms W-2 online and submit them to the SSA by typing your wage information into easy-to-use fill-in fields. In addition, you can print out completed copies of Forms W-2 to file with state or local governments, distribute to your employees, and keep for your records. Form W-3 will be created for you based on your Forms W-2.

Filing Addresses

Generally, your filing address for Forms 940, 941, 943, 944, 945, and CT-1 depends on the location of your residence or principal place of business and whether or not you are including a payment with your return. There are separate filing addresses for these returns if you are a tax-exempt organization or government entity. See the separate instructions for Forms 940, 941, 943, 944, 945, or CT-1 for the filing addresses.

Dishonored Payments

Any form of payment that is dishonored and returned from a financial institution is subject to a penalty. The penalty is $25 or 2% of the payment, whichever is more. However, the penalty on dishonored payments of $24.99 or less is an amount equal to the payment. For example, a dishonored payment of $18 is charged a penalty of $18.

Photographs of Missing Children

The IRS is a proud partner with the National Center for Missing and Exploited Children. Photographs of missing children selected by the Center may appear in this publication on pages that would otherwise be blank. You can help bring these children home by looking at the photographs and calling 1-800-THE-LOST (1-800-843-5678) if you recognize a child.

Calendar

The following is a list of important dates. Also see Pub. 509, Tax Calendars.

 If any date shown next for filing a return, furnishing a form, or depositing taxes falls on a Saturday, Sunday, or legal holiday, use the next business day. A statewide legal holiday delays a filing due date only if the IRS office where you are required to file is located in that state. However, a statewide legal holiday doesn't delay the due date of federal tax deposits. See Deposits on Business Days Only *in section 11. For any filing due date, you will meet the "file" or "furnish" requirement if the envelope containing the return or form is properly addressed, contains sufficient postage, and is postmarked by the U.S. Postal Service on or before the due date, or sent by an IRS-designated private delivery service on or before the due date. See* Private Delivery Services *under* Reminders *for more information.*

By January 31

Furnish Forms 1099 and W-2. Furnish each employee a completed Form W-2. Furnish each other payee a completed Form 1099 (for example, Form 1099-MISC).

File Form 941 or Form 944. File Form 941 for the fourth quarter of the previous calendar year and deposit any undeposited income, social security, and Medicare taxes. You may pay these taxes with Form 941 if your total tax liability for the quarter is less than $2,500. File Form 944 for the previous calendar year instead of Form 941 if the IRS has notified you in writing to file Form 944 and pay any undeposited income, social security, and Medicare taxes. You may pay these taxes with Form 944 if your total tax liability for the year is less than $2,500. For additional rules on when you can pay your taxes with your return, see *Payment with return* in section 11. If you timely deposited all taxes when due, you may file by February 10.

File Form 940. File Form 940 to report any FUTA tax. However if you deposited all of the FUTA tax when due, you may file by February 10.

File Form 945. File Form 945 to report any nonpayroll federal income tax withheld. If you deposited all taxes when due, you may file by February 10. See *Nonpayroll Income Tax Withholding* under *Reminders* for more information.

By February 15

Request a new Form W-4 from exempt employees. Ask for a new Form W-4 from each employee who claimed exemption from income tax withholding last year.

On February 16

Forms W-4 claiming exemption from withholding expire. Any Form W-4 claiming exemption from withholding for the previous year has now expired. Begin withholding for any employee who previously claimed exemption from withholding but hasn't given you a new Form W-4 for the current year. If the employee doesn't give you a new Form W-4, withhold tax based on the last valid Form W-4 you have for the employee that doesn't claim exemption from withholding or, if one doesn't exist, as if he or she is single with zero withholding allowances. See section 9 for more information. If the employee furnishes a new Form W-4 claiming exemption from withholding after February 15, you may apply the exemption to future wages, but don't refund taxes withheld while the exempt status wasn't in place.

 Both paper and electronically filed 2016 Forms W-2 and W-3 must be filed with the SSA by January 31, 2017. Both paper and electronically filed 2016 Form 1099-MISC must be filed with the IRS by January 31, 2017.

By February 28

File paper 2015 Forms 1099 and 1096. File Copy A of all paper 2015 Forms 1099 with Form 1096, Annual Summary and Transmittal of U.S. Information Returns, with the IRS. For electronically filed returns, see *By March 31* below.

By February 29

File paper 2015 Forms W-2 and W-3. File Copy A of all paper 2015 Forms W-2 with Form W-3, Transmittal of Wage and Tax Statements, with the SSA. For electronically filed returns, see *By March 31* below.

File paper Form 8027. File paper Form 8027, Employer's Annual Information Return of Tip Income and Allocated Tips, with the IRS. See section 6. For electronically filed returns, see *By March 31* next.

By March 31

File electronic 2015 Forms 1099, 8027, and W-2. File electronic 2015 Forms 1099 and 8027 with the IRS. File electronic 2015 Forms W-2 with the SSA. For information on reporting Form W-2 information to the SSA electronically, visit the Social Security Administration's Employer W-2 Filing Instructions & Information webpage at *www.socialsecurity.gov/employer*. For information on filing information returns electronically with the IRS, see Pub. 1220, Specifications for Electronic Filing of Forms 1097, 1098, 1099, 3921, 3922, 5498, 8935, and W-2G; and Pub. 1239, Specifications for Electronic Filing of Form 8027, Employer's Annual Information Return of Tip Income and Allocated Tips.

By April 30, July 31, October 31, and January 31

Deposit FUTA taxes. Deposit FUTA tax due if it is more than $500.

File Form 941. File Form 941 and deposit any undeposited income, social security, and Medicare taxes. You may pay these taxes with Form 941 if your total tax liability for the quarter is less than $2,500. If you timely deposited all taxes when due, you may file by May 10, August 10, November 10, or February 10, respectively.

Before December 1

New Forms W-4. Remind employees to submit a new Form W-4 if their marital status or withholding allowances have changed or will change for the next year.

Introduction

This publication explains your tax responsibilities as an employer. It explains the requirements for withholding, depositing, reporting, paying, and correcting employment taxes. It explains the forms you must give to your employees, those your employees must give to you, and those you must send to the IRS and SSA. This guide also has tax tables you need to figure the taxes to withhold from each employee for 2016. References to "income tax" in this guide apply only to "federal" income tax. Contact your state or local tax department to determine if their rules are different.

When you pay your employees, you don't pay them all the money they earned. As their employer, you have the added responsibility of withholding taxes from their paychecks. The federal income tax and employees' share of social security and Medicare taxes that you withhold from your employees' paychecks are part of their wages that you pay to the United States Treasury instead of to your employees. Your employees trust that you pay the withheld taxes to the United States Treasury by making federal tax deposits. This is the reason that these withheld taxes are called trust fund taxes. If federal income, social security, or Medicare taxes that must be withheld aren't withheld or aren't deposited or paid to the United States Treasury, the trust fund recovery penalty may apply. See section 11 for more information.

Additional employment tax information is available in Pub. 15-A. Pub. 15-A includes specialized information supplementing the basic employment tax information provided in this publication. Pub. 15-B, Employer's Tax Guide to Fringe Benefits, contains information about the employment tax treatment and valuation of various types of noncash compensation.

Most employers must withhold (except FUTA), deposit, report, and pay the following employment taxes.

- Income tax.

- Social security tax.

- Medicare tax.

- FUTA tax.

There are exceptions to these requirements. See section 15 for guidance. Railroad retirement taxes are explained in the Instructions for Form CT-1.

Comments and suggestions. We welcome your comments about this publication and your suggestions for future editions. You can send us comments from www.irs.gov/formspubs. Click on *More Information* and then click on *Give us feedback*.

Or you can write to:

Internal Revenue Service
Tax Forms and Publications
1111 Constitution Ave. NW, IR-6526
Washington, DC 20224

We respond to many letters by telephone. Therefore, it would be helpful if you would include your daytime phone number, including the area code, in your correspondence.

Although we can't respond individually to each comment received, we do appreciate your feedback and will consider your comments as we revise our tax forms, instructions, and publications.

Federal Government employers. The information in this publication, including the rules for making federal tax deposits, applies to federal agencies.

State and local government employers. Payments to employees for services in the employ of state and local government employers are generally subject to federal income tax withholding but not FUTA tax. Most elected and appointed public officials of state or local governments are employees under common law rules. See chapter 3 of Pub. 963, Federal-State Reference Guide. In addition, wages, with certain exceptions, are subject to social security and Medicare taxes. See section 15 for more information on the exceptions.

If an election worker is employed in another capacity with the same government entity, see Revenue Ruling 2000-6 on page 512 of Internal Revenue Bulletin 2000-6 at www.irs.gov/pub/irs-irbs/irb00-06.pdf.

You can get information on reporting and social security coverage from your local IRS office. If you have any questions about coverage under a section 218 (Social Security Act) agreement, contact the appropriate state official. To find your State Social Security Administrator, visit the National Conference of State Social Security Administrators website at www.ncsssa.org.

Disregarded entities and qualified subchapter S subsidiaries (QSubs). Eligible single-owner disregarded entities and QSubs are treated as separate entities for employment tax purposes. Eligible single-member entities that haven't elected to be taxed as corporations must report and pay employment taxes on wages paid to their employees using the entities' own names and EINs. See Regulations sections 1.1361-4(a)(7) and 301.7701-2(c)(2)(iv).

COBRA premium assistance credit. The Consolidated Omnibus Budget Reconciliation Act of 1985 (COBRA) provides certain former employees, retirees, spouses, former spouses, and dependent children the right to temporary continuation of health coverage at group rates. COBRA generally covers multiemployer health plans and health plans maintained by private-sector employers (other than churches) with 20 or more full and part-time employees. Parallel requirements apply to these plans under the Employee Retirement Income Security Act of 1974 (ERISA). Under the Public Health Service Act, COBRA requirements apply also to health plans covering state or local government employees. Similar requirements apply under the Federal Employees Health Benefits Program and under some state laws. For the premium assistance (or subsidy) discussed below, these requirements are all referred to as COBRA requirements.

Under the American Recovery and Reinvestment Act of 2009 (ARRA), employers are allowed a credit against "payroll taxes" (referred to in this publication as "employment taxes") for providing COBRA premium assistance to assistance eligible individuals. For periods of COBRA continuation coverage beginning after February 16, 2009, a group health plan must treat an assistance eligible individual as having paid the required COBRA continuation coverage premium if the individual elects COBRA coverage and pays 35% of the amount of the premium.

An assistance eligible individual is a qualified beneficiary of an employer's group health plan who is eligible for COBRA continuation coverage during the period beginning September 1, 2008, and ending May 31, 2010, due to the involuntarily termination from employment of a covered employee during the period and elects continuation COBRA coverage. The assistance for the coverage can last up to 15 months.

Employees terminated during the period beginning September 1, 2008, and ending May 31, 2010, who received a severance package that delayed the start of the COBRA continuation coverage, may still be eligible for premium assistance for COBRA continuation coverage. For more information see Notice 2009-27, 2009-16 I.R.B. 838, available at www.irs.gov/irb/2009-16_irb/ar09.html.

Administrators of the group health plans (or other entities) that provide or administer COBRA continuation coverage must provide notice to assistance eligible individuals of the COBRA premium assistance.

The 65% of the premium not paid by the assistance eligible individuals is reimbursed to the employer maintaining the group health plan. The reimbursement is made through a credit against the employer's employment tax liabilities. For information on how to claim the credit, see the Instructions for Form 941-X or the Instructions for Form 944-X. The credit is treated as a deposit made on the first day of the return period (quarter or year). In the case of a multiemployer plan, the credit is claimed by the plan, rather than the employer. In the case of an insured plan subject to state law continuation coverage requirements, the credit is claimed by the insurance company, rather than the employer.

Anyone claiming the credit for COBRA premium assistance payments must maintain the following information to support their claim, including the following.

- Information on the receipt of the assistance eligible individuals' 35% share of the premium, including dates and amounts.

- In the case of an insurance plan, a copy of invoice or other supporting statement from the insurance carrier and proof of timely payment of the full premium to the insurance carrier required under COBRA.

- In the case of a self-insured plan, proof of the premium amount and proof of the coverage provided to the assistance eligible individuals.

- Attestation of involuntary termination, including the date of the involuntary termination for each covered employee whose involuntary termination is the basis for eligibility for the subsidy.

- Proof of each assistance eligible individual's eligibility for COBRA coverage and the election of COBRA coverage.

- A record of the SSNs of all covered employees, the amount of the subsidy reimbursed with respect to each covered employee, and whether the subsidy was for one individual or two or more individuals.

For more information, visit IRS.gov and enter "COBRA" in the search box.

1. Employer Identification Number (EIN)

If you are required to report employment taxes or give tax statements to employees or annuitants, you need an EIN.

The EIN is a nine-digit number the IRS issues. The digits are arranged as follows: 00-0000000. It is used to identify the tax accounts of employers and certain others who have no employees. Use your EIN on all of the items you send to the IRS and SSA. For more information, see Pub. 1635.

If you don't have an EIN, you may apply for one online. Visit IRS.gov and enter "EIN" in the search box. You may also apply for an EIN by faxing or mailing Form SS-4 to the IRS. Employers outside of the United States may also apply for an EIN by calling 267-941-1099 (toll call). Don't use an SSN in place of an EIN.

You should have only one EIN. If you have more than one and aren't sure which one to use, call 1-800-829-4933 or 1-800-829-4059 (TDD/TTY for persons who are deaf, hard of hearing, or have a speech disability). Give the numbers you have, the name and address to which each was assigned, and the address of your main place of business. The IRS will tell you which number to use.

If you took over another employer's business (see *Successor employer* in section 9), don't use that employer's EIN. If you have applied for an EIN but don't have your EIN by the time a return is due, file a paper return and write "Applied For" and the date you applied for it in the space shown for the number.

2. Who Are Employees?

Generally, employees are defined either under common law or under statutes for certain situations. See Pub. 15-A for details on statutory employees and nonemployees.

Employee status under common law. Generally, a worker who performs services for you is your employee if you have the right to control what will be done and how it will be done. This is so even when you give the employee freedom of action. What matters is that you have the right to control the details of how the services are performed. See Pub. 15-A for more information on how to determine whether an individual providing services is an independent contractor or an employee.

Generally, people in business for themselves aren't employees. For example, doctors, lawyers, veterinarians, and others in an independent trade in which they offer their services to the public are usually not employees. However, if the business is incorporated, corporate officers who work in the business are employees of the corporation.

If an employer-employee relationship exists, it doesn't matter what it is called. The employee may be called an agent or independent contractor. It also doesn't matter how payments are measured or paid, what they are called, or if the employee works full or part time.

Statutory employees. If someone who works for you isn't an employee under the common law rules discussed above, don't withhold federal income tax from his or her pay, unless backup withholding applies. Although the following persons may not be common law employees, they are considered employees by statute for social security, Medicare, and FUTA tax purposes under certain conditions.

- An agent (or commission) driver who delivers food, beverages (other than milk), laundry, or dry cleaning for someone else.

- A full-time life insurance salesperson who sells primarily for one company.

- A homeworker who works by guidelines of the person for whom the work is done, with materials furnished by and returned to that person or to someone that person designates.

- A traveling or city salesperson (other than an agent-driver or commission-driver) who works full time (except for sideline sales activities) for one firm or person getting orders from customers. The orders must be for merchandise for resale or supplies for use in the customer's business. The customers must be retailers, wholesalers, contractors, or operators of hotels, restaurants, or other businesses dealing with food or lodging.

Statutory nonemployees. Direct sellers, qualified real estate agents, and certain companion sitters are, by law, considered nonemployees. They are generally treated as self-employed for all federal tax purposes, including income and employment taxes.

H-2A agricultural workers. On Form W-2, don't check box 13 (Statutory employee), as H-2A workers aren't statutory employees.

Treating employees as nonemployees. You will generally be liable for social security and Medicare taxes and withheld income tax if you don't deduct and withhold these taxes because you treated an employee as a nonemployee. You may be able to calculate your liability using special IRC section 3509 rates for the employee share of social security and Medicare taxes and the federal income tax withholding. The applicable rates depend on whether you filed required Forms 1099. You can't recover the employee share of social security tax, Medicare tax, or income tax withholding from the employee if the tax is paid under IRC section 3509. You are liable for the income tax withholding regardless of whether the employee paid income tax on the wages. You continue to owe the full employer share of social security and Medicare taxes. The employee remains liable for the employee share of social security and Medicare taxes. See IRC section 3509 for details. Also see the Instructions for Form 941-X.

IRC section 3509 rates aren't available if you intentionally disregard the requirement to withhold taxes from the employee or if you withheld income taxes but not social security or Medicare taxes. IRC section 3509 isn't available for reclassifying statutory employees. See *Statutory employees*, earlier.

If the employer issued required information returns, the IRC section 3509 rates are:

- For social security taxes; employer rate of 6.2% plus 20% of the employee rate (see the Instructions for Form 941-X).
- For Medicare taxes; employer rate of 1.45% plus 20% of the employee rate of 1.45%, for a total rate of 1.74% of wages.
- For Additional Medicare Tax; 0.18% (20% of the employee rate of 0.9%) of wages subject to Additional Medicare Tax.
- For income tax withholding, the rate is 1.5% of wages.

If the employer didn't issue required information returns, the IRC section 3509 rates are:

- For social security taxes; employer rate of 6.2% plus 40% of the employee rate (see the Instructions for Form 941-X).
- For Medicare taxes; employer rate of 1.45% plus 40% of the employee rate of 1.45%, for a total rate of 2.03% of wages.
- For Additional Medicare Tax; 0.36% (40% of the employee rate of 0.9%) of wages subject to Additional Medicare Tax.
- For income tax withholding, the rate is 3.0% of wages.

Relief provisions. If you have a reasonable basis for not treating a worker as an employee, you may be relieved from having to pay employment taxes for that worker. To get this relief, you must file all required federal tax returns, including information returns, on a basis consistent with your treatment of the worker. You (or your predecessor) must not have treated any worker holding a substantially similar position as an employee for any periods beginning after 1977. See Pub. 1976, Do You Qualify for Relief Under Section 530.

IRS help. If you want the IRS to determine whether a worker is an employee, file Form SS-8.

Voluntary Classification Settlement Program (VCSP). Employers who are currently treating their workers (or a class or group of workers) as independent contractors or other nonemployees and want to voluntarily reclassify their workers as employees for future tax periods may be eligible to participate in the VCSP if certain requirements are met. File Form 8952 to apply for the VCSP. For more information visit IRS.gov and enter "VCSP" in the search box.

Business Owned and Operated by Spouses

If you and your spouse jointly own and operate a business and share in the profits and losses, you are partners in a partnership, whether or not you have a formal partnership agreement. See Pub. 541 for more details. The partnership is considered the employer of any employees, and is liable for any employment taxes due on wages paid to its employees.

Exception—Qualified joint venture. For tax years beginning after December 31, 2006, the Small Business and Work Opportunity Tax Act of 2007 (Public Law 110-28) provides that a "qualified joint venture," whose only members are spouses filing a joint income tax return, can elect not to be treated as a partnership for federal tax purposes. A qualified joint venture conducts a trade or business where:

- The only members of the joint venture are spouses who file a joint income tax return,

- Both spouses materially participate (see *Material participation* in the Instructions for Schedule C (Form 1040), line G) in the trade or business (mere joint ownership of property isn't enough),

- Both spouses elect to not be treated as a partnership, and

- The business is co-owned by both spouses and isn't held in the name of a state law entity such as a partnership or limited liability company (LLC).

To make the election, all items of income, gain, loss, deduction, and credit must be divided between the spouses, in accordance with each spouse's interest in the venture, and reported on separate Schedules C or F as sole proprietors. Each spouse must also file a separate Schedule SE to pay self-employment taxes, as applicable.

Spouses using the qualified joint venture rules are treated as sole proprietors for federal tax purposes and generally don't need an EIN. If employment taxes are owed by the qualified joint venture, either spouse may report and pay the employment taxes due on the wages paid to the employees using the EIN of that spouse's sole proprietorship. Generally, filing as a qualified joint venture won't increase the spouses' total tax owed on the joint income tax return. However, it gives each spouse credit for social security earnings on which retirement benefits are based and for Medicare coverage without filing a partnership return.

Note. If your spouse is your employee, not your partner, see *One spouse employed by another* in section 3.

For more information on qualified joint ventures, visit IRS.gov and enter "qualified joint venture" in the search box.

Exception—Community income. If you and your spouse wholly own an unincorporated business as community property under the community property laws of a state, foreign country, or U.S. possession, you can treat the business either as a sole proprietorship (of the spouse who carried on the business) or a partnership. You may still make an election to be taxed as a qualified joint venture instead of a partnership. See *Exception—Qualified joint venture*, earlier.

---

3. Family Employees

Child employed by parents. Payments for the services of a child under age 18 who works for his or her parent in a trade or business aren't subject to social security and Medicare taxes if the trade or business is a sole proprietorship or a partnership in which each partner is a parent of the child. If these payments are for work other than in a trade or business, such as domestic work in the parent's private home, they aren't subject to social security and Medicare taxes until the child reaches age 21. However, see *Covered services of a child or spouse* below. Payments for the services of a child under age 21 who works for his or her parent, whether or not in a trade or business, aren't subject to FUTA tax. Payments for the services of a child of any age who works for his or her parent are gener-

ally subject to income tax withholding unless the payments are for domestic work in the parent's home, or unless the payments are for work other than in a trade or business and are less than $50 in the quarter or the child isn't regularly employed to do such work.

One spouse employed by another. The wages for the services of an individual who works for his or her spouse in a trade or business are subject to income tax withholding and social security and Medicare taxes, but not to FUTA tax. However, the payments for services of one spouse employed by another in other than a trade or business, such as domestic service in a private home, aren't subject to social security, Medicare, and FUTA taxes.

Covered services of a child or spouse. The wages for the services of a child or spouse are subject to income tax withholding as well as social security, Medicare, and FUTA taxes if he or she works for:

- A corporation, even if it is controlled by the child's parent or the individual's spouse;

- A partnership, even if the child's parent is a partner, unless each partner is a parent of the child;

- A partnership, even if the individual's spouse is a partner; or

- An estate, even if it is the estate of a deceased parent.

Parent employed by son or daughter. When the employer is a son or daughter employing his or her parent the following rules apply.

- Payments for the services of a parent in the son's or daughter's (the employer's) trade or business are subject to income tax withholding and social security and Medicare taxes.

- Payments for the services of a parent not in the son's or daughter's (the employer's) trade or business are generally not subject to social security and Medicare taxes.

 Social security and Medicare taxes do apply to payments made to a parent for domestic services if all of the following apply:

- *The parent is employed by his or her son or daughter;*

- *The son or daughter (the employer) has a child or stepchild living in the home;*

- *The son or daughter (the employer) is a widow or widower, divorced, or living with a spouse who, because of a mental or physical condition, can't care for the child or stepchild for at least 4 continuous weeks in a calendar quarter; and*

- *The child or stepchild is either under age 18 or requires the personal care of an adult for at least 4 continuous weeks in a calendar quarter due to a mental or physical condition.*

Payments made to a parent employed by his or her child aren't subject to FUTA tax, regardless of the type of services provided.

4. Employee's Social Security Number (SSN)

You are required to get each employee's name and SSN and to enter them on Form W-2. This requirement also applies to resident and nonresident alien employees. You should ask your employee to show you his or her social security card. The employee may show the card if it is available.

 Don't accept a social security card that says "Not valid for employment." A social security number issued with this legend doesn't permit employment.

You may, but aren't required to, photocopy the social security card if the employee provides it. If you don't provide the correct employee name and SSN on Form W-2, you may owe a penalty unless you have reasonable cause. See Pub. 1586, Reasonable Cause Regulations & Requirements for Missing and Incorrect Name/TINs, for information on the requirement to solicit the employee's SSN.

Applying for a social security card. Any employee who is legally eligible to work in the United States and doesn't have a social security card can get one by completing Form SS-5, Application for a Social Security Card, and submitting the necessary documentation. You can get Form SS-5 from the SSA website at *www.socialsecurity.gov/online/ss-5.html*, at SSA offices, or by calling 1-800-772-1213 or 1-800-325-0778 (TTY). The employee must complete and sign Form SS-5; it can't be filed by the employer. You may be asked to supply a letter to accompany Form SS-5 if the employee has exceeded his or her yearly or lifetime limit for the number of replacement cards allowed.

Applying for an SSN. If you file Form W-2 on paper and your employee applied for an SSN but doesn't have one when you must file Form W-2, enter "Applied For" on the form. If you are filing electronically, enter all zeros (000-00-000) in the SSN field. When the employee receives the SSN, file Copy A of Form W-2c, Corrected Wage and Tax Statement, with the SSA to show the employee's SSN. Furnish copies B, C, and 2 of Form W-2c to the employee. Up to 25 Forms W-2c for each Form W-3c, Transmittal of Corrected Wage and Tax Statements, may now be filed per session over the Internet, with no limit on the number of sessions. For more information, visit the SSA's Employer W-2 Filing Instructions & Information webpage at *www.socialsecurity.gov/employer*. Advise your employee to correct the SSN on his or her original Form W-2.

Correctly record the employee's name and SSN. Record the name and SSN of each employee as they are shown on the employee's social security card. If the employee's name isn't correct as shown on the card (for example, because of marriage or divorce), the employee should request an updated card from the SSA. Continue to report the employee's wages under the old name until the employee shows you the updated social security card with the corrected name.

If the SSA issues the employee an updated card after a name change, or a new card with a different SSN, file a Form W-2c to correct the name/SSN reported for the most recently filed Form W-2. It isn't necessary to correct other years if the previous name and number were used for years before the most recent Form W-2.

IRS individual taxpayer identification numbers (ITINs) for aliens. Don't accept an ITIN in place of an SSN for employee identification or for work. An ITIN is only available to resident and nonresident aliens who aren't eligible for U.S. employment and need identification for other tax purposes. You can identify an ITIN because it is a nine-digit number, formatted like an SSN, that starts with the number "9" and has a range of numbers from "70–88", "90–92", and "94–99" for the fourth and fifth digits (for example, 9NN-7N-NNNN).

 An individual with an ITIN who later becomes eligible to work in the United States must obtain an SSN. If the individual is currently eligible to work in the United States, instruct the individual to apply for an SSN and follow the instructions under Applying for an SSN above. Don't use an ITIN in place of an SSN on Form W-2.

Verification of SSNs. Employers and authorized reporting agents can use the Social Security Number Verification Service (SSNVS) to instantly verify up to 10 names and SSNs (per screen) at a time, or submit an electronic file of up to 250,000 names and SSNs and usually receive the results the next business day. Visit *www.socialsecurity.gov/employer/ssnv.htm* for more information.

Registering for SSNVS. You must register online and receive authorization from your employer to use SSNVS. To register, visit SSA's website at *www.socialsecurity.gov/bso* and click on the *Register* link under *Business Services Online*. Follow the registration instructions to obtain a user identification (ID) and password. You will need to provide the following information about yourself and your company.

- Name.

- SSN.

- Date of birth.

- Type of employer.

- EIN.

- Company name, address, and telephone number.

- Email address.

When you have completed the online registration process, SSA will mail a one-time activation code to your employer. You must enter the activation code online to use SSNVS.

5. Wages and Other Compensation

Wages subject to federal employment taxes generally include all pay you give to an employee for services performed. The pay may be in cash or in other forms. It includes salaries, vacation allowances, bonuses, commissions, and fringe benefits. It doesn't matter how you measure or make the payments. Amounts an employer pays as a bonus for signing or ratifying a contract in connection with the establishment of an employer-employee relationship and an amount paid to an employee for cancellation of an employment contract and relinquishment of contract rights are wages subject to social security, Medicare, and FUTA taxes and income tax withholding. Also, compensation paid to a former employee for services performed while still employed is wages subject to employment taxes.

More information. See section 6 for a discussion of tips and section 7 for a discussion of supplemental wages. Also, see section 15 for exceptions to the general rules for wages. Pub. 15-A provides additional information on wages, including nonqualified deferred compensation, and other compensation. Pub. 15-B provides information on other forms of compensation, including:

- Accident and health benefits,

- Achievement awards,

- Adoption assistance,

- Athletic facilities,

- De minimis (minimal) benefits,

- Dependent care assistance,

- Educational assistance,

- Employee discounts,

- Employee stock options,

- Employer-provided cell phones,

- Group-term life insurance coverage,

- Health Savings Accounts,

- Lodging on your business premises,

- Meals,

- Moving expense reimbursements,

- No-additional-cost services,

- Retirement planning services,

- Transportation (commuting) benefits,

- Tuition reduction, and

- Working condition benefits.

Employee business expense reimbursements. A reimbursement or allowance arrangement is a system by which you pay the advances, reimbursements, and charges for your employees' business expenses. How you report a reimbursement or allowance amount depends on whether you have an accountable or a nonaccountable plan. If a single payment includes both wages and an expense reimbursement, you must specify the amount of the reimbursement.

These rules apply to all ordinary and necessary employee business expenses that would otherwise qualify for a deduction by the employee.

Accountable plan. To be an accountable plan, your reimbursement or allowance arrangement must require your employees to meet all three of the following rules.

1. They must have paid or incurred deductible expenses while performing services as your employees. The reimbursement or advance must be payment for the expenses and must not be an amount that would have otherwise been paid to the employee as wages.

2. They must substantiate these expenses to you within a reasonable period of time.

3. They must return any amounts in excess of substantiated expenses within a reasonable period of time.

Amounts paid under an accountable plan aren't wages and aren't subject to income, social security, Medicare, and FUTA taxes.

If the expenses covered by this arrangement aren't substantiated (or amounts in excess of substantiated expenses aren't returned within a reasonable period of time), the amount paid under the arrangement in excess of the substantiated expenses is treated as paid under a nonaccountable plan. This amount is subject to income, social security, Medicare, and FUTA taxes for the first payroll period following the end of the reasonable period of time.

A reasonable period of time depends on the facts and circumstances. Generally, it is considered reasonable if your employees receive their advance within 30 days of the time they incur the expenses, adequately account for the expenses within 60 days after the expenses were paid or incurred, and return any amounts in excess of expenses within 120 days after the expenses were paid or incurred. Also, it is considered reasonable if you give your employees a periodic statement (at least quarterly) that asks them to either return or adequately account for outstanding amounts and they do so within 120 days.

Nonaccountable plan. Payments to your employee for travel and other necessary expenses of your business under a nonaccountable plan are wages and are treated as supplemental wages and subject to income, social security, Medicare, and FUTA taxes. Your payments are treated as paid under a nonaccountable plan if:

- Your employee isn't required to or doesn't substantiate timely those expenses to you with receipts or other documentation,

- You advance an amount to your employee for business expenses and your employee isn't required to or doesn't return timely any amount he or she doesn't use for business expenses,

- You advance or pay an amount to your employee regardless of whether you reasonably expect the employee to have business expenses related to your business, or

- You pay an amount as a reimbursement you would have otherwise paid as wages.

See section 7 for more information on supplemental wages.

Per diem or other fixed allowance. You may reimburse your employees by travel days, miles, or some other fixed allowance under the applicable revenue procedure. In these cases, your employee is considered to have accounted to you if your reimbursement doesn't exceed rates established by the Federal Government. The 2015 standard mileage rate for auto expenses was 57.5 cents per mile. The rate for 2016 is 54 cents per mile.

The government per diem rates for meals and lodging in the continental United States can be found by visiting the U.S. General Services Administration website at www.GSA.gov and entering "per diem rates" in the search box. Other than the amount of these expenses, your employees' business expenses must be substantiated (for example, the business purpose of the travel or the number of business miles driven). For information on substantiation methods, see Pub. 463.

If the per diem or allowance paid exceeds the amounts substantiated, you must report the excess amount as wages. This excess amount is subject to income tax withholding and payment of social security, Medicare, and FUTA taxes. Show the amount equal to the substantiated amount (for example, the nontaxable portion) in box 12 of Form W-2 using code "L."

Wages not paid in money. If in the course of your trade or business you pay your employees in a medium that is neither cash nor a readily negotiable instrument, such as a check, you are said to pay them "in kind." Payments in kind may be in the form of goods, lodging, food, clothing, or services. Generally, the fair market value of such payments at the time they are provided is subject to federal income tax withholding and social security, Medicare, and FUTA taxes.

However, noncash payments for household work, agricultural labor, and service not in the employer's trade or business are exempt from social security, Medicare, and FUTA taxes. Withhold income tax on these payments only if you and the employee agree to do so. Nonetheless, noncash payments for agricultural labor, such as commodity wages, are treated as cash payments subject to employment taxes if the substance of the transaction is a cash payment.

Moving expenses. Reimbursed and employer-paid qualified moving expenses (those that would otherwise be deductible by the employee) paid under an accountable plan aren't includible in an employee's income unless you have knowledge the employee deducted the expenses in a prior year. Reimbursed and employer-paid nonqualified moving expenses are includible in income and are subject to employment taxes and income tax withholding. For more information on moving expenses, see Pub. 521.

Meals and lodging. The value of meals isn't taxable income and isn't subject to income tax withholding and social security, Medicare, and FUTA taxes if the meals are furnished for the employer's convenience and on the employer's premises. The value of lodging isn't subject to income tax withholding and social security, Medicare, and FUTA taxes if the lodging is furnished for the employer's convenience, on the employer's premises, and as a condition of employment.

"For the convenience of the employer" means you have a substantial business reason for providing the meals and lodging other than to provide additional compensation to the employee. For example, meals you provide at the place of work so that an employee is available for emergencies during his or her lunch period are generally considered to be for your convenience.

However, whether meals or lodging are provided for the convenience of the employer depends on all of the facts and circumstances. A written statement that the meals or lodging are for your convenience isn't sufficient.

50% test. If over 50% of the employees who are provided meals on an employer's business premises receive these meals for the convenience of the employer, all meals provided on the premises are treated as furnished for the convenience of the employer. If this 50% test is met, the value of the meals is excludable from income for all employees and isn't subject to federal income tax withholding or employment taxes. For more information, see Pub. 15-B.

Health insurance plans. If you pay the cost of an accident or health insurance plan for your employees, including an employee's spouse and dependents, your payments aren't wages and aren't subject to social security, Medicare, and FUTA taxes, or federal income tax withholding. Generally, this exclusion also applies to qualified long-term care insurance contracts. However, for income tax withholding, the value of health insurance benefits must be included in the wages of S corporation employees who own more than 2% of the S corporation (2% shareholders). For social security, Medicare, and FUTA taxes, the health insurance benefits are excluded from the wages only for employees and their dependents or for a class or classes of employees and their dependents. See Announcement 92-16 for more information. You can find

Announcement 92-16 on page 53 of Internal Revenue Bulletin 1992-5.

Health Savings Accounts and medical savings accounts. Your contributions to an employee's Health Savings Account (HSA) or Archer medical savings account (MSA) aren't subject to social security, Medicare, or FUTA taxes, or federal income tax withholding if it is reasonable to believe at the time of payment of the contributions they will be excludable from the income of the employee. To the extent it isn't reasonable to believe they will be excludable, your contributions are subject to these taxes. Employee contributions to their HSAs or MSAs through a payroll deduction plan must be included in wages and are subject to social security, Medicare, and FUTA taxes and income tax withholding. However, HSA contributions made under a salary reduction arrangement in a section 125 cafeteria plan aren't wages and aren't subject to employment taxes or withholding. For more information, see the Instructions for Form 8889.

Medical care reimbursements. Generally, medical care reimbursements paid for an employee under an employer's self-insured medical reimbursement plan aren't wages and aren't subject to social security, Medicare, and FUTA taxes, or income tax withholding. See Pub. 15-B for an exception for highly compensated employees.

Differential wage payments. Differential wage payments are any payments made by an employer to an individual for a period during which the individual is performing service in the uniformed services while on active duty for a period of more than 30 days and represent all or a portion of the wages the individual would have received from the employer if the individual were performing services for the employer.

Differential wage payments are wages for income tax withholding, but aren't subject to social security, Medicare, or FUTA taxes. Employers should report differential wage payments in box 1 of Form W-2. For more information about the tax treatment of differential wage payments, visit IRS.gov and enter "employees in a combat zone" in the search box.

Fringe benefits. You generally must include fringe benefits in an employee's gross income (but see *Nontaxable fringe benefits* next). The benefits are subject to income tax withholding and employment taxes. Fringe benefits include cars you provide, flights on aircraft you provide, free or discounted commercial flights, vacations, discounts on property or services, memberships in country clubs or other social clubs, and tickets to entertainment or sporting events. In general, the amount you must include is the amount by which the fair market value of the benefits is more than the sum of what the employee paid for it plus any amount the law excludes. There are other special rules you and your employees may use to value certain fringe benefits. See Pub. 15-B for more information.

Nontaxable fringe benefits. Some fringe benefits aren't taxable (or are minimally taxable) if certain conditions are met. See Pub. 15-B for details. The following are some examples of nontaxable fringe benefits.

1. Services provided to your employees at no additional cost to you.

2. Qualified employee discounts.

3. Working condition fringes that are property or services the employee could deduct as a business expense if he or she had paid for it. Examples include a company car for business use and subscriptions to business magazines.

4. Certain minimal value fringes (including an occasional cab ride when an employee must work overtime and meals you provide at eating places you run for your employees if the meals aren't furnished at below cost).

5. Qualified transportation fringes subject to specified conditions and dollar limitations (including transportation in a commuter highway vehicle, any transit pass, and qualified parking).

6. Qualified moving expense reimbursement. See *Moving expenses*, earlier in this section, for details.

7. The use of on-premises athletic facilities, if substantially all of the use is by employees, their spouses, and their dependent children.

8. Qualified tuition reduction an educational organization provides to its employees for education. For more information, see Pub. 970.

9. Employer-provided cell phones provided primarily for a noncompensatory business reason.

However, don't exclude the following fringe benefits from the income of highly compensated employees unless the benefit is available to other employees on a nondiscriminatory basis.

- No-additional-cost services.

- Qualified employee discounts.

- Meals provided at an employer operated eating facility.

- Reduced tuition for education.

For more information, including the definition of a highly compensated employee, see Pub. 15-B.

When fringe benefits are treated as paid. You may choose to treat certain noncash fringe benefits as paid by the pay period, by the quarter, or on any other basis you choose as long as you treat the benefits as paid at least once a year. You don't have to make a formal choice of payment dates or notify the IRS of the dates you choose. You don't have to make this choice for all employees. You may change methods as often as you like, as long as you treat all benefits provided in a calendar year as paid by December 31 of the calendar year. See Pub. 15-B for more information, including a discussion of the special accounting rule for fringe benefits provided during November and December.

Valuation of fringe benefits. Generally, you must determine the value of fringe benefits no later than January

31 of the next year. Before January 31, you may reasonably estimate the value of the fringe benefits for purposes of withholding and depositing on time.

Withholding on fringe benefits. You may add the value of fringe benefits to regular wages for a payroll period and figure withholding taxes on the total, or you may withhold federal income tax on the value of the fringe benefits at the optional flat 25% supplemental wage rate. However, see *Withholding on supplemental wages when an employee receives more than $1 million of supplemental wages during the calendar year* in section 7.

You may choose not to withhold income tax on the value of an employee's personal use of a vehicle you provide. You must, however, withhold social security and Medicare taxes on the use of the vehicle. See Pub. 15-B for more information on this election.

Depositing taxes on fringe benefits. Once you choose when fringe benefits are paid, you must deposit taxes in the same deposit period you treat the fringe benefits as paid. To avoid a penalty, deposit the taxes following the general deposit rules for that deposit period.

If you determine by January 31 you overestimated the value of a fringe benefit at the time you withheld and deposited for it, you may claim a refund for the overpayment or have it applied to your next employment tax return. See *Valuation of fringe benefits*, earlier. If you underestimated the value and deposited too little, you may be subject to a failure-to-deposit (FTD) penalty. See section 11 for information on deposit penalties.

If you deposited the required amount of taxes but withheld a lesser amount from the employee, you can recover from the employee the social security, Medicare, or income taxes you deposited on his or her behalf, and included in the employee's Form W-2. However, you must recover the income taxes before April 1 of the following year.

Sick pay. In general, sick pay is any amount you pay under a plan to an employee who is unable to work because of sickness or injury. These amounts are sometimes paid by a third party, such as an insurance company or an employees' trust. In either case, these payments are subject to social security, Medicare, and FUTA taxes. These taxes don't apply to sick pay paid more than 6 calendar months after the last calendar month in which the employee worked for the employer. The payments are always subject to federal income tax. See Pub. 15-A for more information.

6. Tips

Tips your employee receives from customers are generally subject to withholding. Your employee must report cash tips to you by the 10th of the month after the month the tips are received. The report should include tips you paid over to the employee for charge customers, tips the employee received directly from customers, and tips received from other employees under any tip-sharing arrangement. Both directly and indirectly tipped employees

must report tips to you. No report is required for months when tips are less than $20. Your employee reports the tips on Form 4070 or on a similar statement. The statement must be signed by the employee and must include:

- The employee's name, address, and SSN,

- Your name and address,

- The month and year (or the beginning and ending dates, if the statement is for a period of less than 1 calendar month) the report covers, and

- The total of tips received during the month or period.

Both Forms 4070 and 4070-A, Employee's Daily Record of Tips, are included in Pub. 1244, Employee's Daily Record of Tips and Report to Employer.

 You are permitted to establish a system for electronic tip reporting by employees. See Regulations section 31.6053-1(d).

Collecting taxes on tips. You must collect income tax, employee social security tax, and employee Medicare tax on the employee's tips. The withholding rules for withholding an employee's share of Medicare tax on tips also apply to withholding the Additional Medicare Tax once wages and tips exceed $200,000 in the calendar year.

You can collect these taxes from the employee's wages or from other funds he or she makes available. See *Tips treated as supplemental wages* in section 7 for more information. Stop collecting the employee social security tax when his or her wages and tips for tax year 2016 reach $118,500; collect the income and employee Medicare taxes for the whole year on all wages and tips. You are responsible for the employer social security tax on wages and tips until the wages (including tips) reach the limit. You are responsible for the employer Medicare tax for the whole year on all wages and tips. File Form 941 or Form 944 to report withholding and employment taxes on tips.

Ordering rule. If, by the 10th of the month after the month for which you received an employee's report on tips, you don't have enough employee funds available to deduct the employee tax, you no longer have to collect it. If there aren't enough funds available, withhold taxes in the following order.

1. Withhold on regular wages and other compensation.

2. Withhold social security and Medicare taxes on tips.

3. Withhold income tax on tips.

Reporting tips. Report tips and any collected and uncollected social security and Medicare taxes on Form W-2 and on Form 941, lines 5b, 5c, and 5d (Form 944, lines 4b, 4c, and 4d). Report an adjustment on Form 941, line 9 (Form 944, line 6), for the uncollected social security and Medicare taxes. Enter the amount of uncollected social security tax and Medicare tax on Form W-2, box 12, with codes "A" and "B." Don't include any uncollected Additional Medicare Tax in box 12 of Form W-2. For additional information on reporting tips, see section 13 and the General Instructions for Forms W-2 and W-3.

Revenue Ruling 2012-18 provides guidance for employers regarding social security and Medicare taxes imposed on tips, including information on the reporting of the employer share of social security and Medicare taxes under section 3121(q), the difference between tips and service charges, and the section 45B credit. See Revenue Ruling 2012-18, 2012-26 I.R.B. 1032, available at www.irs.gov/irb/2012-26_IRB/ar07.html.

FUTA tax on tips. If an employee reports to you in writing $20 or more of tips in a month, the tips are also subject to FUTA tax.

Allocated tips. If you operate a large food or beverage establishment, you must report allocated tips under certain circumstances. However, don't withhold income, social security, or Medicare taxes on allocated tips.

A large food or beverage establishment is one that provides food or beverages for consumption on the premises, where tipping is customary, and where there were normally more than 10 employees on a typical business day during the preceding year.

The tips may be allocated by one of three methods—hours worked, gross receipts, or good faith agreement. For information about these allocation methods, including the requirement to file Forms 8027 electronically if 250 or more forms are filed, see the Instructions for Form 8027. For information on filing Form 8027 electronically with the IRS, see Pub. 1239.

Tip Rate Determination and Education Program. Employers may participate in the Tip Rate Determination and Education Program. The program primarily consists of two voluntary agreements developed to improve tip income reporting by helping taxpayers to understand and meet their tip reporting responsibilities. The two agreements are the Tip Rate Determination Agreement (TRDA) and the Tip Reporting Alternative Commitment (TRAC). A tip agreement, the Gaming Industry Tip Compliance Agreement (GITCA), is available for the gaming (casino) industry. To get more information about TRDA and TRAC agreements, see Pub. 3144. Additionally, visit IRS.gov and enter "MSU tips" in the search box to get more information about GITCA, TRDA, or TRAC agreements.

7. Supplemental Wages

Supplemental wages are wage payments to an employee that aren't regular wages. They include, but aren't limited to, bonuses, commissions, overtime pay, payments for accumulated sick leave, severance pay, awards, prizes, back pay, retroactive pay increases, and payments for nondeductible moving expenses. Other payments subject to the supplemental wage rules include taxable fringe benefits and expense allowances paid under a nonaccountable plan. How you withhold on supplemental wages depends on whether the supplemental payment is identified as a separate payment from regular wages. See Regulations section 31.3402(g)-1 for additional guidance for wages paid after January 1, 2007. Also see Revenue

Ruling 2008-29, 2008-24 I.R.B. 1149, available at www.irs.gov/irb/2008-24_IRB/ar08.html.

Withholding on supplemental wages when an employee receives more than $1 million of supplemental wages from you during the calendar year. Special rules apply to the extent supplemental wages paid to any one employee during the calendar year exceed $1 million. If a supplemental wage payment, together with other supplemental wage payments made to the employee during the calendar year, exceeds $1 million, the excess is subject to withholding at 39.6% (or the highest rate of income tax for the year). Withhold using the 39.6% rate without regard to the employee's Form W-4. In determining supplemental wages paid to the employee during the year, include payments from all businesses under common control. For more information, see Treasury Decision 9276, 2006-37 I.R.B. 423, available at www.irs.gov/irb/2006-37_IRB/ar09.html.

Withholding on supplemental wage payments to an employee who doesn't receive $1 million of supplemental wages during the calendar year. If the supplemental wages paid to the employee during the calendar year are less than or equal to $1 million, the following rules apply in determining the amount of income tax to be withheld.

Supplemental wages combined with regular wages. If you pay supplemental wages with regular wages but don't specify the amount of each, withhold federal income tax as if the total were a single payment for a regular payroll period.

Supplemental wages identified separately from regular wages. If you pay supplemental wages separately (or combine them in a single payment and specify the amount of each), the federal income tax withholding method depends partly on whether you withhold income tax from your employee's regular wages.

1. If you withheld income tax from an employee's regular wages in the current or immediately preceding calendar year, you can use one of the following methods for the supplemental wages.

   a. Withhold a flat 25% (no other percentage allowed).

   b. If the supplemental wages are paid concurrently with regular wages, add the supplemental wages to the concurrently paid regular wages. If there are no concurrently paid regular wages, add the supplemental wages to alternatively, either the regular wages paid or to be paid for the current payroll period or the regular wages paid for the preceding payroll period. Figure the income tax withholding as if the total of the regular wages and supplemental wages is a single payment. Subtract the tax withheld from the regular wages. Withhold the remaining tax from the supplemental wages. If there were other payments of supplemental wages paid during the payroll period made before the current payment of supplemental wages, aggregate all the payments of supplemental wages paid during the payroll period with the regular wages paid during the payroll period, calculate the tax on the total, subtract the tax already withheld from the regular wages and the previous supplemental wage payments, and withhold the remaining tax.

2. If you didn't withhold income tax from the employee's regular wages in the current or immediately preceding calendar year, use method 1-b. This would occur, for example, when the value of the employee's withholding allowances claimed on Form W-4 is more than the wages.

Regardless of the method you use to withhold income tax on supplemental wages, they are subject to social security, Medicare, and FUTA taxes.

Example 1. You pay John Peters a base salary on the 1st of each month. He is single and claims one withholding allowance. In January he is paid $1,000. Using the wage bracket tables, you withhold $50 from this amount. In February, he receives salary of $1,000 plus a commission of $2,000, which you combine with regular wages and don't separately identify. You figure the withholding based on the total of $3,000. The correct withholding from the tables is $336.

Example 2. You pay Sharon Warren a base salary on the 1st of each month. She is single and claims one allowance. Her May 1 pay is $2,000. Using the wage bracket tables, you withhold $186. On May 14 she receives a bonus of $1,000. Electing to use supplemental wage withholding method 1-b, you:

1. Add the bonus amount to the amount of wages from the most recent base salary pay date (May 1) ($2,000 + $1,000 = $3,000).

2. Determine the amount of withholding on the combined $3,000 amount to be $336 using the wage bracket tables.

3. Subtract the amount withheld from wages on the most recent base salary pay date (May 1) from the combined withholding amount ($336 – $186 = $150).

4. Withhold $150 from the bonus payment.

Example 3. The facts are the same as in Example 2, except you elect to use the flat rate method of withholding on the bonus. You withhold 25% of $1,000, or $250, from Sharon's bonus payment.

Example 4. The facts are the same as in Example 2, except you elect to pay Sharon a second bonus of $2,000 on May 28. Using supplemental wage withholding method 1-b, you:

1. Add the first and second bonus amounts to the amount of wages from the most recent base salary pay date (May 1) ($2,000 + $1,000 + $2,000 = $5,000).

2. Determine the amount of withholding on the combined $5,000 amount to be $771 using the wage bracket tables.

3. Subtract the amounts withheld from wages on the most recent base salary pay date (May 1) and the amounts withheld from the first bonus payment from the combined withholding amount ($771 – $186 – $150 = $435).

4. Withhold $435 from the second bonus payment.

Tips treated as supplemental wages. Withhold income tax on tips from wages earned by the employee or from other funds the employee makes available. If an employee receives regular wages and reports tips, figure income tax withholding as if the tips were supplemental wages. If you haven't withheld income tax from the regular wages, add the tips to the regular wages. Then withhold income tax on the total. If you withheld income tax from the regular wages, you can withhold on the tips by method 1-a or 1-b discussed earlier in this section under *Supplemental wages identified separately from regular wages*.

Vacation pay. Vacation pay is subject to withholding as if it were a regular wage payment. When vacation pay is in addition to regular wages for the vacation period, treat it as a supplemental wage payment. If the vacation pay is for a time longer than your usual payroll period, spread it over the pay periods for which you pay it.

8. Payroll Period

Your payroll period is a period of service for which you usually pay wages. When you have a regular payroll period, withhold income tax for that time period even if your employee doesn't work the full period.

No regular payroll period. When you don't have a regular payroll period, withhold the tax as if you paid wages for a daily or miscellaneous payroll period. Figure the number of days (including Sundays and holidays) in the period covered by the wage payment. If the wages are unrelated to a specific length of time (for example, commissions paid on completion of a sale), count back the number of days from the payment period to the latest of:

- The last wage payment made during the same calendar year,

- The date employment began, if during the same calendar year, or

- January 1 of the same year.

Employee paid for period less than 1 week. When you pay an employee for a period of less than one week, and the employee signs a statement under penalties of perjury indicating he or she isn't working for any other employer during the same week for wages subject to withholding, figure withholding based on a weekly payroll period. If the employee later begins to work for another employer for wages subject to withholding, the employee must notify you within 10 days. You then figure withholding based on the daily or miscellaneous period.

9. Withholding From Employees' Wages

Income Tax Withholding

Using Form W-4 to figure withholding. To know how much federal income tax to withhold from employees' wages, you should have a Form W-4 on file for each employee. Encourage your employees to file an updated Form W-4 for 2016, especially if they owed taxes or received a large refund when filing their 2015 tax return. Advise your employees to use the IRS Withholding Calculator on the IRS website at *www.irs.gov/individuals* for help in determining how many withholding allowances to claim on their Forms W-4.

Ask all new employees to give you a signed Form W-4 when they start work. Make the form effective with the first wage payment. If a new employee doesn't give you a completed Form W-4, withhold income tax as if he or she is single, with no withholding allowances.

Form in Spanish. You can provide Formulario W-4(SP) in place of Form W-4, to your Spanish-speaking employees. For more information, see Pub. 17(SP). The rules discussed in this section that apply to Form W-4 also apply to Formulario W-4(SP).

Electronic system to receive Form W-4. You may establish a system to electronically receive Forms W-4 from your employees. See Regulations section 31.3402(f)(5)-1(c) for more information.

Effective date of Form W-4. A Form W-4 remains in effect until the employee gives you a new one. When you receive a new Form W-4 from an employee, don't adjust withholding for pay periods before the effective date of the new form. If an employee gives you a Form W-4 that replaces an existing Form W-4, begin withholding no later than the start of the first payroll period ending on or after the 30th day from the date when you received the replacement Form W-4. For exceptions, see *Exemption from federal income tax withholding*, *IRS review of requested Forms W-4*, and *Invalid Forms W-4*, later in this section.

 A Form W-4 that makes a change for the next calendar year won't take effect in the current calendar year.

Successor employer. If you are a successor employer (see *Successor employer*, later in this section), secure new Forms W-4 from the transferred employees unless the "Alternative Procedure" in section 5 of Revenue Procedure 2004-53 applies. See Revenue Procedure 2004-53, 2004-34 I.R.B. 320, available at *www.irs.gov/irb/2004-34_IRB/ar13.html*.

Completing Form W-4. The amount of any federal income tax withholding must be based on marital status and withholding allowances. Your employees may not base their withholding amounts on a fixed dollar amount or percentage. However, an employee may specify a dollar amount to be withheld in addition to the amount of withholding based on filing status and withholding allowances claimed on Form W-4.

Employees may claim fewer withholding allowances than they are entitled to claim. They may wish to claim fewer allowances to ensure they have enough withholding or to offset the tax on other sources of taxable income not subject to withholding.

See Pub. 505 for more information about completing Form W-4. Along with Form W-4, you may wish to order Pub. 505 for use by your employees.

Don't accept any withholding or estimated tax payments from your employees in addition to withholding based on their Form W-4. If they require additional withholding, they should submit a new Form W-4 and, if necessary, pay estimated tax by filing Form 1040-ES or by using EFTPS to make estimated tax payments.

Exemption from federal income tax withholding. Generally, an employee may claim exemption from federal income tax withholding because he or she had no income tax liability last year and expects none this year. See the Form W-4 instructions for more information. However, the wages are still subject to social security and Medicare taxes. See also *Invalid Forms W-4*, later in this section.

A Form W-4 claiming exemption from withholding is effective when it is filed with the employer and only for that calendar year. To continue to be exempt from withholding in the next calendar year, an employee must give you a new Form W-4 by February 15. If the employee doesn't give you a new Form W-4 by February 15, begin withholding based on the last Form W-4 for the employee that didn't claim an exemption from withholding or, if one wasn't furnished, then withhold tax as if he or she is single with zero withholding allowances. If the employee provides a new Form W-4 claiming exemption from withholding on February 16 or later, you may apply it to future wages but don't refund any taxes already withheld.

Withholding income taxes on the wages of nonresident alien employees. In general, you must withhold federal income taxes on the wages of nonresident alien employees. However, see Pub. 515 for exceptions to this general rule. Also see section 3 of Pub. 51 for guidance on H-2A visa workers.

Withholding adjustment for nonresident alien employees. Apply the procedure discussed next to figure the amount of income tax to withhold from the wages of nonresident alien employees performing services within the United States.

 Nonresident alien students from India and business apprentices from India aren't subject to this procedure.

Instructions. To figure how much income tax to withhold from the wages paid to a nonresident alien employee performing services in the United States, use the following steps.

Step 1. Add to the wages paid to the nonresident alien employee for the payroll period the amount shown in the chart next for the applicable payroll period.

Amount to Add to Nonresident Alien Employee's Wages for Calculating Income Tax Withholding Only

Payroll Period	Add Additional
Weekly	$ 43.30
Biweekly	86.50
Semimonthly	93.80
Monthly	187.50
Quarterly	562.50
Semiannually	1,125.00
Annually	2,250.00
Daily or Miscellaneous (each day of the payroll period)	8.70

Step 2. Use the amount figured in *Step 1* and the number of withholding allowances claimed (generally limited to one allowance) to figure income tax withholding. Determine the value of withholding allowances by multiplying the number of withholding allowances claimed by the appropriate amount from *Table 5* shown on page 45. If you are using the Percentage Method Tables for Income Tax Withholding, provided on pages 44–45, reduce the amount figured in *Step 1* by the value of withholding allowances and use that reduced amount to figure the income tax withholding. If you are using the Wage Bracket Method Tables for Income Tax Withholding, provided on pages 46–65, use the amount figured in *Step 1* and the number of withholding allowances to figure income tax withholding.

The amounts from the chart, earlier, are added to wages solely for calculating income tax withholding on the wages of the nonresident alien employee. The amounts from the chart shouldn't be included in any box on the employee's Form W-2 and don't increase the income tax liability of the employee. Also, the amounts from the chart don't increase the social security tax or Medicare tax liability of the employer or the employee, or the FUTA tax liability of the employer.

This procedure only applies to nonresident alien employees who have wages subject to income tax withholding.

Example. An employer using the percentage method of withholding pays wages of $500 for a biweekly payroll period to a married nonresident alien employee. The nonresident alien has properly completed Form W-4, entering marital status as "single" with one withholding allowance and indicating status as a nonresident alien on Form W-4, line 6 (see *Nonresident alien employee's Form W-4* below in this section). The employer determines the wages to be used in the withholding tables by adding to the $500

amount of wages paid the amount of $86.50 from the chart under *Step 1* ($586.50 total). The employer then applies the applicable tables to determine the income tax withholding for nonresident aliens (see *Step 2*). **Reminder:** If you use the Percentage Method Tables for Income Tax Withholding, reduce the amount figured in Step 1 by the value of withholding allowances and use that reduced amount to figure income tax withholding.

The $86.50 added to wages for calculating income tax withholding isn't reported on Form W-2, and doesn't increase the income tax liability of the employee. Also, the $86.50 added to wages doesn't affect the social security tax or Medicare tax liability of the employer or the employee, or the FUTA tax liability of the employer.

Supplemental wage payment. This procedure for determining the amount of income tax withholding doesn't apply to a supplemental wage payment (see *section 7*) if the 39.6% mandatory flat rate withholding applies or if the 25% optional flat rate withholding is being used to calculate income tax withholding on the supplemental wage payment.

Nonresident alien employee's Form W-4. When completing Forms W-4, nonresident aliens are required to:

- Not claim exemption from income tax withholding,

- Request withholding as if they are single, regardless of their actual marital status,

- Claim only one allowance (if the nonresident alien is a resident of Canada, Mexico, or South Korea, or a student or business apprentice from India, he or she may claim more than one allowance), and

- Write "Nonresident Alien" or "NRA" above the dotted line on line 6 of Form W-4.

If you maintain an electronic Form W-4 system, you should provide a field for nonresident aliens to enter nonresident alien status instead of writing "Nonresident Alien" or "NRA" above the dotted line on line 6.

 A nonresident alien employee may request additional withholding at his or her option for other purposes, although such additions shouldn't be necessary for withholding to cover federal income tax liability related to employment.

Form 8233. If a nonresident alien employee claims a tax treaty exemption from withholding, the employee must submit Form 8233 with respect to the income exempt under the treaty, instead of Form W-4. See Pub. 515 for details.

IRS review of requested Forms W-4. When requested by the IRS, you must make original Forms W-4 available for inspection by an IRS employee. You may also be directed to send certain Forms W-4 to the IRS. You may receive a notice from the IRS requiring you to submit a copy of Form W-4 for one or more of your named employees. Send the requested copy or copies of Form W-4 to the IRS at the address provided and in the manner directed by the notice. The IRS may also require you to submit copies of Form W-4 to the IRS as directed by Treasury Decision 9337, 2007-35 I.R.B. 455, which is available at *www.irs.gov/irb/2007-35_IRB/ar10.html*. When we refer to Form W-4, the same rules apply to Formulario W-4(SP), its Spanish translation.

After submitting a copy of a requested Form W-4 to the IRS, continue to withhold federal income tax based on that Form W-4 if it is valid (see *Invalid Forms W-4* below in this section). However, if the IRS later notifies you in writing the employee isn't entitled to claim exemption from withholding or a claimed number of withholding allowances, withhold federal income tax based on the effective date, marital status, and maximum number of withholding allowances specified in the IRS notice (commonly referred to as a "lock-in letter").

Initial lock-in letter. The IRS also uses information reported on Form W-2 to identify employees with withholding compliance problems. In some cases, if a serious under-withholding problem is found to exist for a particular employee, the IRS may issue a lock-in letter to the employer specifying the maximum number of withholding allowances and marital status permitted for a specific employee. You will also receive a copy for the employee that identifies the maximum number of withholding allowances permitted and the process by which the employee can provide additional information to the IRS for purposes of determining the appropriate number of withholding allowances. You must furnish the employee copy to the employee within 10 business days of receipt if the employee is employed by you as of the date of the notice. Begin withholding based on the notice on the date specified in the notice.

Employee not performing services. If you receive a notice for an employee who isn't performing services for you, you must still furnish the employee copy to the employee and withhold based on the notice if any of the following apply.

- You are paying wages for the employee's prior services and the wages are subject to income tax withholding on or after the date specified in the notice.

- You reasonably expect the employee to resume services within 12 months of the date of the notice.

- The employee is on a leave of absence that doesn't exceed 12 months or the employee has a right to re-employment after the leave of absence.

Termination and re-hire of employees. If you must furnish and withhold based on the notice and the employment relationship is terminated after the date of the notice, you must continue to withhold based on the notice if you continue to pay any wages subject to income tax withholding. You must also withhold based on the notice or modification notice (explained next) if the employee resumes the employment relationship with you within 12 months after the termination of the employment relationship.

Modification notice. After issuing the notice specifying the maximum number of withholding allowances and marital status permitted, the IRS may issue a subsequent notice (modification notice) that modifies the original notice. The modification notice may change the marital status and/or the number of withholding allowances permitted. You must withhold federal income tax based on the effective date specified in the modification notice.

New Form W-4 after notice. After the IRS issues a notice or modification notice, if the employee provides you with a new Form W-4 claiming complete exemption from withholding or claims a marital status, a number of withholding allowances, and any additional withholding that results in less withholding than would result under the IRS notice or modification notice, disregard the new Form W-4. You must withhold based on the notice or modification notice unless the IRS notifies you to withhold based on the new Form W-4. If the employee wants to put a new Form W-4 into effect that results in less withholding than required, the employee must contact the IRS.

If, after you receive an IRS notice or modification notice, your employee gives you a new Form W-4 that doesn't claim exemption from federal income tax withholding and claims a marital status, a number of withholding allowances, and any additional withholding that results in more withholding than would result under the notice or modification notice, you must withhold tax based on the new Form W-4. Otherwise, disregard any subsequent Forms W-4 provided by the employee and withhold based on the IRS notice or modification notice.

For additional information about these rules, see Treasury Decision 9337, 2007-35 I.R.B. 455, available at *www.irs.gov/irb/2007-35_IRB/ar10.html*.

Substitute Forms W-4. You are encouraged to have your employees use the official version of Form W-4 to claim withholding allowances or exemption from withholding.

You may use a substitute version of Form W-4 to meet your business needs. However, your substitute Form W-4 must contain language that is identical to the official Form W-4 and your form must meet all current IRS rules for substitute forms. At the time you provide your substitute form to the employee, you must provide him or her with all tables, instructions, and worksheets from the current Form W-4.

You can't accept substitute Forms W-4 developed by employees. An employee who submits an employee-developed substitute Form W-4 after October 10, 2007, will be treated as failing to furnish a Form W-4. However, continue to honor any valid employee-developed Forms W-4 you accepted before October 11, 2007.

Invalid Forms W-4. Any unauthorized change or addition to Form W-4 makes it invalid. This includes taking out any language by which the employee certifies the form is correct. A Form W-4 is also invalid if, by the date an employee gives it to you, he or she indicates in any way it is false. An employee who submits a false Form W-4 may be subject to a $500 penalty. You may treat a Form W-4 as invalid if the employee wrote "exempt" on line 7 and also entered a number on line 5 or an amount on line 6.

When you get an invalid Form W-4, don't use it to figure federal income tax withholding. Tell the employee it is invalid and ask for another one. If the employee doesn't give you a valid one, withhold tax as if the employee is single with zero withholding allowances. However, if you have an earlier Form W-4 for this worker that is valid, withhold as you did before.

Amounts exempt from levy on wages, salary, and other income. If you receive a Notice of Levy on Wages, Salary, and Other Income (Forms 668-W(ACS), 668-W(c)(DO), or 668-W(ICS)), you must withhold amounts as described in the instructions for these forms. Pub. 1494 has tables to figure the amount exempt from levy. If a levy issued in a prior year is still in effect and the taxpayer submits a new Statement of Exemptions and Filing Status, use the current year Pub. 1494 to compute the exempt amount.

Social Security and Medicare Taxes

The Federal Insurance Contributions Act (FICA) provides for a federal system of old-age, survivors, disability, and hospital insurance. The old-age, survivors, and disability insurance part is financed by the social security tax. The hospital insurance part is financed by the Medicare tax. Each of these taxes is reported separately.

Generally, you are required to withhold social security and Medicare taxes from your employees' wages and pay the employer's share of these taxes. Certain types of wages and compensation aren't subject to social security and Medicare taxes. See section 5 and section 15 for details. Generally, employee wages are subject to social security and Medicare taxes regardless of the employee's age or whether he or she is receiving social security benefits. If the employee reported tips, see section 6.

Tax rates and the social security wage base limit. Social security and Medicare taxes have different rates and only the social security tax has a wage base limit. The wage base limit is the maximum wage subject to the tax for the year. Determine the amount of withholding for social security and Medicare taxes by multiplying each payment by the employee tax rate. There are no withholding allowances for social security and Medicare taxes.

For 2016, the social security tax rate is 6.2% (amount withheld) each for the employer and employee (12.4% total). The social security wage base limit is $118,500. The tax rate for Medicare is 1.45% (amount withheld) each for the employee and employer (2.9% total). There is no wage base limit for Medicare tax; all covered wages are subject to Medicare tax.

Additional Medicare Tax withholding. In addition to withholding Medicare tax at 1.45%, you must withhold a 0.9% Additional Medicare Tax from wages you pay to an employee in excess of $200,000 in a calendar year. You are required to begin withholding Additional Medicare Tax in the pay period in which you pay wages in excess of $200,000 to an employee and continue to withhold it each pay period until the end of the calendar year. Additional

Medicare Tax is only imposed on the employee. There is no employer share of Additional Medicare Tax. All wages that are subject to Medicare tax are subject to Additional Medicare Tax withholding if paid in excess of the $200,000 withholding threshold.

For more information on what wages are subject to Medicare tax, see the chart, *Special Rules for Various Types of Services and Payments*, in section 15. For more information on Additional Medicare Tax, visit IRS.gov and enter "Additional Medicare Tax" in the search box.

Successor employer. When corporate acquisitions meet certain requirements, wages paid by the predecessor are treated as if paid by the successor for purposes of applying the social security wage base and for applying the Additional Medicare Tax withholding threshold (that is, $200,000 in a calendar year). You should determine whether or not you should file Schedule D (Form 941), Report of Discrepancies Caused by Acquisitions, Statutory Mergers, or Consolidations, by reviewing the Instructions for Schedule D (Form 941). See Regulations section 31.3121(a)(1)-1(b) for more information. Also see Revenue Procedure 2004-53, 2004-34 I.R.B. 320, available at *www.irs.gov/irb/2004-34_IRB/ar13.html*.

Example. Early in 2016, you bought all of the assets of a plumbing business from Mr. Martin. Mr. Brown, who had been employed by Mr. Martin and received $2,000 in wages before the date of purchase, continued to work for you. The wages you paid to Mr. Brown are subject to social security taxes on the first $116,500 ($118,500 minus $2,000). Medicare tax is due on all of the wages you pay him during the calendar year. You should include the $2,000 Mr. Brown received while employed by Mr. Martin in determining whether Mr. Brown's wages exceed the $200,000 for Additional Medicare Tax withholding threshold.

Withholding of social security and Medicare taxes on nonresident aliens. In general, if you pay wages to nonresident alien employees, you must withhold federal social security and Medicare taxes as you would for a U.S. citizen. However, see Pub. 515 for exceptions to this general rule.

International social security agreements. The United States has social security agreements, also known as totalization agreements, with many countries that eliminate dual taxation and dual coverage. Compensation subject to social security and Medicare taxes may be exempt under one of these agreements. You can get more information and a list of agreement countries from the SSA at *www.socialsecurity.gov/international* or see section 7 of Pub. 15-A.

Religious exemption. An exemption from social security and Medicare taxes is available to members of a recognized religious sect opposed to insurance. This exemption is available only if both the employee and the employer are members of the sect. For more information, see Pub. 517.

Foreign persons treated as American employers. Under IRC section 3121(z), for services performed after July 31, 2008, a foreign person who meets both of the following conditions is generally treated as an American employer for purposes of paying FICA taxes on wages paid to an employee who is a United States citizen or resident.

1. The foreign person is a member of a domestically controlled group of entities.

2. The employee of the foreign person performs services in connection with a contract between the U.S. Government (or an instrumentality of the U.S. Government) and any member of the domestically controlled group of entities. Ownership of more than 50% constitutes control.

Part-Time Workers

Part-time workers and workers hired for short periods of time are treated the same as full-time employees, for federal income tax withholding and social security, Medicare, and FUTA tax purposes.

Generally, it doesn't matter whether the part-time worker or worker hired for a short period of time has another job or has the maximum amount of social security tax withheld by another employer. See *Successor employer*, earlier, for an exception to this rule.

Income tax withholding may be figured the same way as for full-time workers or it may be figured by the part-year employment method explained in section 9 of Pub. 15-A.

10. Required Notice to Employees About the Earned Income Credit (EIC)

You must notify employees who have no federal income tax withheld that they may be able to claim a tax refund because of the EIC. Although you don't have to notify employees who claim exemption from withholding on Form W-4 about the EIC, you are encouraged to notify any employees whose wages for 2015 were less than $47,747 ($53,267 if married filing jointly) that they may be eligible to claim the credit for 2015. This is because eligible employees may get a refund of the amount of EIC that is more than the tax they owe.

You will meet this notification requirement if you issue the employee Form W-2 with the EIC notice on the back of Copy B, or a substitute Form W-2 with the same statement. You will also meet the requirement by providing Notice 797, Possible Federal Tax Refund Due to the Earned Income Credit (EIC), or your own statement that contains the same wording.

If a substitute for Form W-2 is given to the employee on time but doesn't have the required statement, you must notify the employee within 1 week of the date the substitute for Form W-2 is given. If Form W-2 is required but isn't given on time, you must give the employee Notice 797 or your written statement by the date Form W-2 is required to be given. If Form W-2 isn't required, you must notify the employee by February 8, 2016.

11. Depositing Taxes

In general, you must deposit federal income tax withheld and both the employer and employee social security and Medicare taxes. You must use EFT to make all federal tax deposits. See *How To Deposit*, later in this section, for information on electronic deposit requirements.

 The credit against employment taxes for COBRA assistance payments is treated as a deposit of taxes on the first day of your return period. See COBRA premium assistance credit *under* Introduction *for more information.*

Payment with return. You may make a payment with Form 941 or Form 944 instead of depositing, without incurring a penalty, if one of the following applies.

- Your Form 941 total tax liability for either the current quarter or the preceding quarter is less than $2,500, and you didn't incur a $100,000 next-day deposit obligation during the current quarter. If you aren't sure your total tax liability for the current quarter will be less than $2,500, (and your liability for the preceding quarter wasn't less than $2,500), make deposits using the semi-weekly or monthly rules so you won't be subject to an FTD penalty.

- You are a monthly schedule depositor (defined later) and make a payment in accordance with the *Accuracy of Deposits Rule*, discussed later in this section. This payment may be $2,500 or more.

Employers who have been notified to file Form 944 can pay their fourth quarter tax liability with Form 944 if the fourth quarter tax liability is less than $2,500. Employers must have deposited any tax liability due for the first, second, and third quarters according to the deposit rules to avoid an FTD penalty for deposits during those quarters.

Separate deposit requirements for nonpayroll (Form 945) tax liabilities. Separate deposits are required for nonpayroll and payroll income tax withholding. Don't combine deposits for Forms 941 (or Form 944) and Form 945 tax liabilities. Generally, the deposit rules for nonpayroll liabilities are the same as discussed next, except the rules apply to an annual rather than a quarterly return period. Thus, the $2,500 threshold for the deposit requirement discussed above applies to Form 945 on an annual basis. See the separate Instructions for Form 945 for more information.

When To Deposit

There are two deposit schedules—monthly and semi-weekly—for determining when you deposit social security,

Medicare, and withheld income taxes. These schedules tell you when a deposit is due after a tax liability arises (for example, when you have a payday). Before the beginning of each calendar year, you must determine which of the two deposit schedules you are required to use. The deposit schedule you must use is based on the total tax liability you reported on Form 941 during a lookback period, discussed next. Your deposit schedule isn't determined by how often you pay your employees or make deposits. See special rules for Forms 944 and 945, later. Also see *Application of Monthly and Semiweekly Schedules*, later in this section.

 These rules don't apply to FUTA tax. See section 14 for information on depositing FUTA tax.

Lookback period. If you are a Form 941 filer, your deposit schedule for a calendar year is determined from the total taxes reported on Forms 941, line 10, in a 4-quarter lookback period. The lookback period begins July 1 and ends June 30 as shown next in Table 1. If you reported $50,000 or less of taxes for the lookback period, you are a monthly schedule depositor; if you reported more than $50,000, you are a semiweekly schedule depositor.

Table 1. Lookback Period for Calendar Year 2016

July 1, 2014 through Sep. 30, 2014	Oct. 1, 2014 through Dec. 31, 2014	Jan. 1, 2015 through Mar. 31, 2015	Apr.1, 2015 through June 30, 2015

 The lookback period for a 2016 Form 941 filer who filed Form 944 in either 2014 or 2015 is calendar year 2014.

If you are a Form 944 filer for the current year or either of the preceding 2 years, your deposit schedule for a calendar year is determined from the total taxes reported during the second preceding calendar year (either on your Form 941 for all 4 quarters of that year or your Form 944 for that year). The lookback period for 2016 for a Form 944 filer is calendar year 2014. If you reported $50,000 or less of taxes for the lookback period, you are a monthly schedule depositor; if you reported more than $50,000, you are a semiweekly schedule depositor.

If you are a Form 945 filer, your deposit schedule for a calendar year is determined from the total taxes reported on line 3 of your Form 945 for the second preceding calendar year. The lookback period for 2016 for a Form 945 filer is calendar year 2014.

Adjustments and the lookback rule. Adjustments made on Form 941-X, Form 944-X, and Form 945-X don't affect the amount of tax liability for previous periods for purposes of the lookback rule.

Example. An employer originally reported a tax liability of $45,000 for the lookback period. The employer discovered, during January 2016, that the tax reported for one of the lookback period quarters was understated by $10,000 and corrected this error by filing Form 941-X. This

employer is a monthly schedule depositor for 2016 because the lookback period tax liabilities are based on the amounts originally reported, and they were $50,000 or less.

Deposit period. The term deposit period refers to the period during which tax liabilities are accumulated for each required deposit due date. For monthly schedule depositors, the deposit period is a calendar month. The deposit periods for semiweekly schedule depositors are Wednesday through Friday and Saturday through Tuesday.

Monthly Deposit Schedule

You are a monthly schedule depositor for a calendar year if the total taxes on Form 941, line 10, for the 4 quarters in your lookback period were $50,000 or less. Under the monthly deposit schedule, deposit employment taxes on payments made during a month by the 15th day of the following month. See also *Deposits on Business Days Only* and the *$100,000 Next-Day Deposit Rule*, later in this section. Monthly schedule depositors shouldn't file Form 941 or Form 944 on a monthly basis.

New employers. Your tax liability for any quarter in the lookback period before you started or acquired your business is considered to be zero. Therefore, you are a monthly schedule depositor for the first calendar year of your business. However, see the *$100,000 Next-Day Deposit Rule*, later in this section.

Semiweekly Deposit Schedule

You are a semiweekly schedule depositor for a calendar year if the total taxes on Form 941, line 10, during your lookback period were more than $50,000. Under the semiweekly deposit schedule, deposit employment taxes for payments made on Wednesday, Thursday, and/or Friday by the following Wednesday. Deposit taxes for payments made on Saturday, Sunday, Monday, and/or Tuesday by the following Friday. See also *Deposits on Business Days Only*, later.

Note. Semiweekly schedule depositors must complete Schedule B (Form 941), Report of Tax Liability for Semiweekly Schedule Depositors, and submit it with Form 941. If you file Form 944 and are a semiweekly schedule depositor, complete Form 945-A, Annual Record of Federal Tax Liability, and submit it with your return (instead of Schedule B).

Table 2. Semiweekly Deposit Schedule

IF the payday falls on a . . .	THEN deposit taxes by the following . . .
Wednesday, Thursday, and/or Friday	Wednesday
Saturday, Sunday, Monday, and/or Tuesday	Friday

Semiweekly deposit period spanning 2 quarters. If you have more than one pay date during a semiweekly period and the pay dates fall in different calendar quarters, you will need to make **separate deposits** for the separate liabilities.

Example. If you have a pay date on Thursday, March 31, 2016 (first quarter), and another pay date on Friday, April 1, 2016 (second quarter), two separate deposits would be required even though the pay dates fall within the same semiweekly period. Both deposits would be due Wednesday, April 6, 2016.

Summary of Steps to Determine Your Deposit Schedule

1. Identify your lookback period (see *Lookback period*, earlier in this section).
2. Add the total taxes you reported on Form 941, line 10, during the lookback period.
3. Determine if you are a monthly or semiweekly schedule depositor:

If the total taxes you reported in the lookback period were	Then you are a . . . .
$50,000 or less	Monthly Schedule Depositor
More than $50,000	Semiweekly Schedule Depositor

Example of Monthly and Semiweekly Schedules

Rose Co. reported Form 941 taxes as follows:

2015 Lookback Period		2016 Lookback Period	
3rd Quarter 2013	$12,000	3rd Quarter 2014	$12,000
4th Quarter 2013	12,000	4th Quarter 2014	12,000
1st Quarter 2014	12,000	1st Quarter 2015	12,000
2nd Quarter 2014	12,000	2nd Quarter 2015	15,000
	$48,000		$51,000

Rose Co. is a monthly schedule depositor for 2015 because its tax liability for the 4 quarters in its lookback period (third quarter 2013 through second quarter 2014) wasn't more than $50,000. However, for 2016, Rose Co. is a semiweekly schedule depositor because the total taxes exceeded $50,000 for the 4 quarters in its lookback period (third quarter 2014 through second quarter 2015).

Deposits on Business Days Only

If a deposit is required to be made on a day that isn't a business day, the deposit is considered timely if it is made by the close of the next business day. A business day is any day other than a Saturday, Sunday, or legal holiday. For example, if a deposit is required to be made on a Friday and Friday is a legal holiday, the deposit will be considered timely if it is made by the following Monday (if that Monday is a business day).

Semiweekly schedule depositors have at least 3 business days to make a deposit. If any of the 3 weekdays

after the end of a semiweekly period is a legal holiday, you will have an additional day for each day that is a legal holiday to make the required deposit. For example, if a semiweekly schedule depositor accumulated taxes for payments made on Friday and the following Monday is a legal holiday, the deposit normally due on Wednesday may be made on Thursday (this allows 3 business days to make the deposit).

Legal holiday. The term "legal holiday" means any legal holiday in the District of Columbia. Legal holidays for 2016 are listed next.

- January 1— New Year's Day
- January 18— Birthday of Martin Luther King, Jr.
- February 15— Washington's Birthday
- April 15— District of Columbia Emancipation Day (observed)
- May 30— Memorial Day
- July 4— Independence Day
- September 5— Labor Day
- October 10— Columbus Day
- November 11— Veterans' Day
- November 24— Thanksgiving Day
- December 26— Christmas Day (observed)

Application of Monthly and Semiweekly Schedules

The terms "monthly schedule depositor" and "semiweekly schedule depositor" don't refer to how often your business pays its employees or even how often you are required to make deposits. The terms identify which set of deposit rules you must follow when an employment tax liability arises. The deposit rules are based on the dates when wages are paid (for example, cash basis); not on when tax liabilities are accrued for accounting purposes.

Monthly schedule example. Spruce Co. is a monthly schedule depositor with seasonal employees. It paid wages each Friday during May but didn't pay any wages during June. Under the monthly deposit schedule, Spruce Co. must deposit the combined tax liabilities for the May paydays by June 15. Spruce Co. doesn't have a deposit requirement for June (due by July 15) because no wages were paid and, therefore, it didn't have a tax liability for June.

Semiweekly schedule example. Green, Inc. is a semiweekly schedule depositor and pays wages once each month on the last Friday of the month. Although Green, Inc., has a semiweekly deposit schedule, it will deposit just once a month because it pays wages only once a month. The deposit, however, will be made under the semiweekly deposit schedule as follows: Green, Inc.'s tax liability for the April 29, 2016 (Friday), payday must be deposited by May 4, 2016 (Wednesday). Under the semiweekly deposit schedule, liabilities for wages paid on Wednesday through Friday must be deposited by the following Wednesday.

$100,000 Next-Day Deposit Rule

If you accumulate $100,000 or more in taxes on any day during a monthly or semiweekly deposit period (see *Deposit period*, earlier in this section), you must deposit the tax by the next business day, whether you are a monthly or semiweekly schedule depositor.

For purposes of the $100,000 rule, don't continue accumulating a tax liability after the end of a deposit period. For example, if a semiweekly schedule depositor has accumulated a liability of $95,000 on a Tuesday (of a Saturday-through-Tuesday deposit period) and accumulated a $10,000 liability on Wednesday, the $100,000 next-day deposit rule doesn't apply. Thus, $95,000 must be deposited by Friday and $10,000 must be deposited by the following Wednesday.

However, once you accumulate at least $100,000 in a deposit period, stop accumulating at the end of that day and begin to accumulate anew on the next day. For example, Fir Co. is a semiweekly schedule depositor. On Monday, Fir Co. accumulates taxes of $110,000 and must deposit this amount on Tuesday, the next business day. On Tuesday, Fir Co. accumulates additional taxes of $30,000. Because the $30,000 isn't added to the previous $110,000 and is less than $100,000, Fir Co. must deposit the $30,000 by Friday (following the semiweekly deposit schedule).

 If you are a monthly schedule depositor and accumulate a $100,000 tax liability on any day, you become a semiweekly schedule depositor on the next day and remain so for at least the rest of the calendar year and for the following calendar year.

Example. Elm, Inc., started its business on May 1, 2016. On Wednesday, May 4, it paid wages for the first time and accumulated a tax liability of $40,000. On Friday, May 6, Elm, Inc., paid wages and accumulated a liability of $60,000, bringing its total accumulated tax liability to $100,000. Because this was the first year of its business, the tax liability for its lookback period is considered to be zero, and it would be a monthly schedule depositor based on the lookback rules. However, since Elm, Inc., accumulated a $100,000 liability on May 6, it became a semiweekly schedule depositor on May 7. It will be a semiweekly schedule depositor for the remainder of 2016 and for 2017. Elm, Inc., is required to deposit the $100,000 by Monday, May 9, the next business day.

Accuracy of Deposits Rule

You are required to deposit 100% of your tax liability on or before the deposit due date. However, penalties won't be applied for depositing less than 100% if both of the following conditions are met.

- Any deposit shortfall doesn't exceed the greater of $100 or 2% of the amount of taxes otherwise required to be deposited.
- The deposit shortfall is paid or deposited by the shortfall makeup date as described next.

Makeup Date for Deposit Shortfall:

1. **Monthly schedule depositor.** Deposit the shortfall or pay it with your return by the due date of your return for the return period in which the shortfall occurred. You may pay the shortfall with your return even if the amount is $2,500 or more.

2. **Semiweekly schedule depositor.** Deposit by the earlier of:

   a. The first Wednesday or Friday (whichever comes first) that falls on or after the 15th of the month following the month in which the shortfall occurred, or

   b. The due date of your return (for the return period of the tax liability).

For example, if a semiweekly schedule depositor has a deposit shortfall during June 2016, the shortfall makeup date is July 15, 2016 (Friday). However, if the shortfall occurred on the required April 1, 2016 (Friday), deposit due date for a March 29, 2016 (Tuesday), pay date, the return due date for the March 29, 2016, pay date (May 2, 2016) would come before the May 18, 2016 (Wednesday), shortfall makeup date. In this case, the shortfall must be deposited by May 2, 2016.

How To Deposit

You must deposit employment taxes, including Form 945 taxes, by EFT. See *Payment with return*, earlier in this section, for exceptions explaining when taxes may be paid with the tax return instead of being deposited.

Electronic deposit requirement. You must use EFT to make all federal tax deposits (such as deposits of employment tax, excise tax, and corporate income tax). Generally, an EFT is made using EFTPS. If you don't want to use EFTPS, you can arrange for your tax professional, financial institution, payroll service, or other trusted third party to make electronic deposits on your behalf. EFTPS is a free service provided by the Department of Treasury. To get more information about EFTPS or to enroll in EFTPS, visit *www.eftps.gov*, or call 1-800-555-4477 or 1-800-733-4829 (TDD). Additional information about EFTPS is also available in Pub. 966.

When you receive your EIN. If you are a new employer that indicated a federal tax obligation when requesting an EIN, you will be pre-enrolled in EFTPS. You will receive information about Express Enrollment in your Employer Identification Number (EIN) Package and an additional mailing containing your EFTPS personal identification number (PIN) and instructions for activating your PIN. Call the toll-free number located in your "How to Activate Your Enrollment" brochure to activate your enrollment and begin making your payroll tax deposits. If you outsource any of your payroll and related tax duties to a third party payer, such as a PSP or reporting agent, be sure to tell them about your EFTPS enrollment.

Deposit record. For your records, an EFT Trace Number will be provided with each successful payment. The number can be used as a receipt or to trace the payment.

Depositing on time. For deposits made by EFTPS to be on time, you must submit the deposit by 8 p.m. Eastern time the day before the date the deposit is due. If you use a third party to make a deposit on your behalf, they may have different cutoff times.

Same-day wire payment option. If you fail to submit a deposit transaction on EFTPS by 8 p.m. Eastern time the day before the date a deposit is due, you can still make your deposit on time by using the Federal Tax Collection Service (FTCS). To use the same-day wire payment method, you will need to make arrangements with your financial institution ahead of time. Please check with your financial institution regarding availability, deadlines, and costs. Your financial institution may charge you a fee for payments made this way. To learn more about the information you will need to provide to your financial institution to make a same-day wire payment, visit the IRS website at *www.irs.gov/payments* and click on *Same-day wire.*

How to claim credit for overpayments. If you deposited more than the right amount of taxes for a quarter, you can choose on Form 941 for that quarter (or on Form 944 for that year) to have the overpayment refunded or applied as a credit to your next return. Don't ask EFTPS to request a refund from the IRS for you.

Deposit Penalties

 Although the deposit penalties information provided next refers specifically to Form 941, these rules also apply to Form 945 and Form 944 (if the employer required to file Form 944 doesn't qualify for the exception to the deposit requirements discussed under Payment with return, *earlier in this section).*

Penalties may apply if you don't make required deposits on time or if you make deposits for less than the required amount. The penalties don't apply if any failure to make a proper and timely deposit was due to reasonable cause and not to willful neglect. If you receive a penalty notice, you can provide an explanation of why you believe reasonable cause exists. The IRS may also waive penalties if you inadvertently fail to deposit in the first quarter you were required to deposit any employment tax, or in the first quarter during which your frequency of deposits changed, if you timely filed your employment tax return.

For amounts not properly or timely deposited, the penalty rates are as follows.

2% -	Deposits made 1 to 5 days late.
5% -	Deposits made 6 to 15 days late.
10% -	Deposits made 16 or more days late. Also applies to amounts paid within 10 days of the date of the first notice the IRS sent asking for the tax due.
10% -	Amounts (that should have been deposited) paid directly to the IRS, or paid with your tax return. But see *Payment with return*, earlier in this section, for an exception.
15% -	Amounts still unpaid more than 10 days after the date of the first notice the IRS sent asking for the tax due or the day on which you received notice and demand for immediate payment, whichever is earlier.

Late deposit penalty amounts are determined using calendar days, starting from the due date of the liability.

Special rule for former Form 944 filers. If you filed Form 944 for the prior year and file Forms 941 for the current year, the FTD penalty won't apply to a late deposit of employment taxes for January of the current year if the taxes are deposited in full by March 15 of the current year.

Order in which deposits are applied. Deposits generally are applied to the most recent tax liability within the quarter. If you receive an FTD penalty notice, you may designate how your deposits are to be applied in order to minimize the amount of the penalty if you do so within 90 days of the date of the notice. Follow the instructions on the penalty notice you received. For more information on designating deposits, see Revenue Procedure 2001-58. You can find Revenue Procedure 2001-58 on page 579 of Internal Revenue Bulletin 2001-50 at *www.irs.gov/pub/irs-irbs/irb01-50.pdf*.

Example. Cedar, Inc. is required to make a deposit of $1,000 on May 15 and $1,500 on June 15. It doesn't make the deposit on May 15. On June 15, Cedar, Inc. deposits $2,000. Under the deposits rule, which applies deposits to the most recent tax liability, $1,500 of the deposit is applied to the June 15 deposit and the remaining $500 is applied to the May deposit. Accordingly, $500 of the May 15 liability remains undeposited. The penalty on this under-deposit will apply as explained above.

Trust fund recovery penalty. If federal income, social security, or Medicare taxes that must be withheld aren't withheld or aren't deposited or paid to the United States Treasury, the trust fund recovery penalty may apply. The penalty is the full amount of the unpaid trust fund tax. This penalty may apply to you if these unpaid taxes can't be immediately collected from the employer or business.

The trust fund recovery penalty may be imposed on all persons who are determined by the IRS to be responsible for collecting, accounting for, or paying over these taxes, and who acted willfully in not doing so.

A **responsible person** can be an officer or employee of a corporation, a partner or employee of a partnership, an accountant, a volunteer director/trustee, or an employee of a sole proprietorship, or any other person or entity that is responsible for collecting, accounting for, or paying over trust fund taxes. A responsible person also may include one who signs checks for the business or otherwise has authority to cause the spending of business funds.

Willfully means voluntarily, consciously, and intentionally. A responsible person acts willfully if the person knows the required actions of collecting, accounting for, or paying over trust fund taxes aren't taking place, or recklessly disregards obvious and known risks to the government's right to receive trust fund taxes.

Separate accounting when deposits aren't made or withheld taxes aren't paid. Separate accounting may be required if you don't pay over withheld employee social security, Medicare, or income taxes; deposit required taxes; make required payments; or file tax returns. In this case, you would receive written notice from the IRS requiring you to deposit taxes into a special trust account for the U.S. Government.

 You may be charged with criminal penalties if you don't comply with the special bank deposit requirements for the special trust account for the U.S. Government.

"Averaged" FTD penalty. IRS may assess an "averaged" FTD penalty of 2% to 10% if you are a monthly schedule depositor and didn't properly complete Form 941, line 14, when your tax liability shown on Form 941, line 10, equaled or exceeded $2,500.

The IRS may also assess an "averaged" FTD penalty of 2% to 10% if you are a semiweekly schedule depositor and your tax liability shown on Form 941, line 10, equaled or exceeded $2,500 and you:

- Completed Form 941, line 14, instead of Schedule B (Form 941);
- Failed to attach a properly completed Schedule B (Form 941); or
- Improperly completed Schedule B (Form 941) by, for example, entering tax deposits instead of tax liabilities in the numbered spaces.

The FTD penalty is figured by distributing your total tax liability shown on Form 941, line 10, equally throughout the tax period. As a result, your deposits and payments may not be counted as timely because the actual dates of your tax liabilities can't be accurately determined.

You can avoid an "averaged" FTD penalty by reviewing your return before you file it. Follow these steps before submitting your Form 941.

- If you are a monthly schedule depositor, report your tax liabilities (not your deposits) in the monthly entry spaces on Form 941, line 14.
- If you are a semiweekly schedule depositor, report your tax liabilities (not your deposits) on Schedule B (Form 941) in the lines that represent the dates your employees were paid.
- Verify your total liability shown on Form 941, line 14, or the bottom of Schedule B (Form 941) equals your tax liability shown on Form 941, line 10.
- Don't show negative amounts on Form 941, line 14, or Schedule B (Form 941).

- For prior period errors don't adjust your tax liabilities reported on Form 941, line 14, or on Schedule B (Form 941). Instead, file an adjusted return (Form 941-X, 944-X, or 945-X) if you are also adjusting your tax liability. If you are only adjusting your deposits in response to an FTD penalty notice, see the Instructions for Schedule B (Form 941) or the Instructions for Form 945-X (for Forms 944 and 945).

12. Filing Form 941 or Form 944

Form 941. Each quarter, if you pay wages subject to income tax withholding (including withholding on sick pay and supplemental unemployment benefits) or social security and Medicare taxes you must file Form 941 unless you receive an IRS notification that you are required to file Form 944 or the following exceptions apply. Also, if you are required to file Form 941 but believe your employment taxes for the calendar year will be $1,000 or less, you may request to file Form 944 instead of Forms 941. See the Instructions for Form 941 for details. Form 941 must be filed by the last day of the month that follows the end of the quarter. See the *Calendar*, earlier.

Form 944. If you receive written notification you qualify for the Form 944 program, you must file Form 944 instead of Form 941. If you received this notification, but prefer to file Form 941, you can request to have your filing requirement changed to Form 941 if you satisfy certain requirements. See the Instructions for Form 944 for details. Employers who must file Form 944 have until the last day of the month that follows the end of the year to file Form 944.

Exceptions. The following exceptions apply to the filing requirements for Forms 941 and 944.

- **Seasonal employers who no longer file for quarters when they regularly have no tax liability because they have paid no wages.** To alert the IRS you won't have to file a return for one or more quarters during the year, check the "Seasonal employer" box on Form 941, line 16. When you fill out Form 941, be sure to check the box on the top of the form that corresponds to the quarter reported. Generally, the IRS won't inquire about unfiled returns if at least one taxable return is filed each year. However, you must check the "Seasonal employer" box on **every** Form 941 you file. Otherwise, the IRS will expect a return to be filed for each quarter.
- **Household employers reporting social security and Medicare taxes and/or withheld income tax.** If you are a sole proprietor and file Form 941 or Form 944 for business employees, you may include taxes for household employees on your Form 941 or Form 944. Otherwise, report social security and Medicare taxes and income tax withholding for household employees on Schedule H (Form 1040). See Pub. 926 for more information.

- **Employers reporting wages for employees in American Samoa, Guam, the Commonwealth of the Northern Mariana Islands, the U.S. Virgin Islands, or Puerto Rico.** If your employees aren't subject to U.S. income tax withholding, use Forms 941-SS, 944, or Formulario 944(SP). Employers in Puerto Rico use Formularios 941-PR, 944(SP), or Form 944. If you have both employees who are subject to U.S. income tax withholding and employees who aren't subject to U.S. income tax withholding, you must file only Form 941 (or Form 944 or Formulario 944(SP)) and include all of your employees' wages on that form. For more information, see Pub. 80, Federal Tax Guide for Employers in U.S. Virgin Islands, Guam, American Samoa, and the Commonwealth of the Northern Mariana Islands, or Pub. 179, Guía Contributiva Federal para Patronos Puertorriqueños.

- **Agricultural employers reporting social security, Medicare, and withheld income taxes.** Report these taxes on Form 943. For more information, see Pub. 51.

Form 941 e-file. The Form 941 e-file program allows a taxpayer to electronically file Form 941 or Form 944 using a computer with an internet connection and commercial tax preparation software. For more information, visit the IRS website at *www.irs.gov/efile*, or call 1-866-255-0654.

Electronic filing by reporting agents. Reporting agents filing Forms 941 or Form 944 for groups of taxpayers can file them electronically. See *Reporting Agents* in section 7 of Pub. 15-A.

Penalties. For each whole or part month a return isn't filed when required (disregarding any extensions of the filing deadline), there is a failure-to-file (FTF) penalty of 5% of the unpaid tax due with that return. The maximum penalty is generally 25% of the tax due. Also, for each whole or part month the tax is paid late (disregarding any extensions of the payment deadline), there is a failure-to-pay (FTP) penalty of 0.5% per month of the amount of tax. For individual filers only, the FTP penalty is reduced from 0.5% per month to 0.25% per month if an installment agreement is in effect. You must have filed your return on or before the due date of the return to qualify for the reduced penalty. The maximum amount of the FTP penalty is also 25% of the tax due. If both penalties apply in any month, the FTF penalty is reduced by the amount of the FTP penalty. The penalties won't be charged if you have a reasonable cause for failing to file or pay. If you receive a penalty notice, you can provide an explanation of why you believe reasonable cause exists.

Note. In addition to any penalties, interest accrues from the due date of the tax on any unpaid balance.

If income, social security, or Medicare taxes that must be withheld aren't withheld or aren't paid, you may be personally liable for the trust fund recovery penalty. See *Trust fund recovery penalty* in section 11.

Use of a third party payer, such as a PSP or reporting agent, doesn't relieve an employer of the responsibility to ensure tax returns are filed and all taxes are paid or deposited correctly and on time.

Don't file more than one Form 941 per quarter or more than one Form 944 per year. Employers with multiple locations or divisions must file only one Form 941 per quarter or one Form 944 per year. Filing more than one return may result in processing delays and may require correspondence between you and the IRS. For information on making adjustments to previously filed returns, see section 13.

Reminders about filing.

- Don't report more than 1 calendar quarter on a Form 941.

- If you need Form 941 or Form 944, get one from the IRS in time to file the return when due. See *Ordering Employer Tax Forms and Publications*, earlier.

- Enter your name and EIN on Form 941 or Form 944. Be sure they are exactly as they appeared on earlier returns.

- See the Instructions for Form 941 or the Instructions for Form 944 for information on preparing the form.

Final return. If you go out of business, you must file a final return for the last quarter (last year for Form 944) in which wages are paid. If you continue to pay wages or other compensation for periods following termination of your business, you must file returns for those periods. See the Instructions for Form 941 or the Instructions for Form 944 for details on how to file a final return.

If you are required to file a final return, you are also required to furnish Forms W-2 to your employees by the due date of your final return. File Forms W-2 and W-3 with the SSA by the last day of the month that follows the due date of your final return. Don't send an original or copy of your Form 941 or Form 944 to the SSA. See the General Instructions for Forms W-2 and W-3 for more information.

Filing late returns for previous years. If possible, get a copy of Form 941 or Form 944 (and separate instructions) with a revision date showing the year for which your delinquent return is being filed. See *Ordering Employer Tax Forms and Publications*, earlier. Contact the IRS at 1-800-829-4933 if you have any questions about filing late returns.

Table 3. **Social Security and Medicare Tax Rates** *(for 3 prior years)*

Calendar Year	Wage Base Limit (each employee)	Tax Rate on Taxable Wages and Tips
2015–Social Security	$118,500	12.4%
2015–Medicare	All Wages	2.9%
2014–Social Security	$117,000	12.4%
2014–Medicare	All Wages	2.9%
2013–Social Security	$113,700	12.4%
2013–Medicare	All Wages	2.9%

Reconciling Forms W-2, W-3, and 941 or 944. When there are discrepancies between Forms 941 or Form 944 filed with the IRS and Forms W-2 and W-3 filed with the SSA, the IRS must contact you to resolve the discrepancies.

Take the following steps to help reduce discrepancies.

1. Report bonuses as wages and as social security and Medicare wages on Forms W-2 and on Form 941 or Form 944.

2. Report both social security and Medicare wages and taxes separately on Forms W-2, W-3, 941, and 944.

3. Report employee share of social security taxes on Form W-2 in the box for social security tax withheld (box 4), not as social security wages.

4. Report employee share of Medicare taxes on Form W-2 in the box for Medicare tax withheld (box 6), not as Medicare wages.

5. Make sure the social security wage amount for each employee doesn't exceed the annual social security wage base limit (for example, $118,500 for 2016).

6. Don't report noncash wages that aren't subject to social security or Medicare taxes as social security or Medicare wages.

7. If you used an EIN on any Form 941 or Form 944 for the year that is different from the EIN reported on Form W-3, enter the other EIN on Form W-3 in the box for "Other EIN used this year" (box h).

8. Be sure the amounts on Form W-3 are the total of amounts from Forms W-2.

9. Reconcile Form W-3 with your four quarterly Forms 941 or annual Form 944 by comparing amounts reported for:

   a. Income tax withholding;

   b. Social security wages, social security tips, and Medicare wages and tips. Form W-3 should include Forms 941 or Form 944 adjustments only for the current year; and

   c. Social security and Medicare taxes.

Don't report backup withholding or withholding on non-payroll payments, such as pensions, annuities, and gambling winnings, on Form 941 or Form 944. Withholding on nonpayroll payments is reported on Forms 1099 or W-2G and must be reported on Form 945. Only taxes and withholding reported on Form W-2 should be reported on Form 941 or Form 944.

Amounts reported on Forms W-2, W-3, and Forms 941 or Form 944 may not match for valid reasons. If they don't match, you should determine the reasons they are valid. Keep your reconciliation so you will have a record of why amounts didn't match in case there are inquiries from the IRS or the SSA. See the Instructions for Schedule D (Form 941) if you need to explain any discrepancies that were caused by an acquisition, statutory merger, or consolidation.

13. Reporting Adjustments to Form 941 or Form 944

Current Period Adjustments

In certain cases, amounts reported as social security and Medicare taxes on Form 941, lines 5a–5d, column 2 (Form 944, lines 4a–4d, column 2), must be adjusted to arrive at your correct tax liability (for example, excluding amounts withheld by a third party payor or amounts you weren't required to withhold). Current period adjustments are reported on Form 941, lines 7–9, or Form 944, line 6, and include the following types of adjustments.

Fractions-of-cents adjustment. If there is a small difference between total taxes after adjustments (Form 941, line 10; Form 944, line 7) and total deposits (Form 941, line 11; Form 944, line 10), it may have been caused, all or in part, by rounding to the nearest cent each time you computed payroll. This rounding occurs when you figure the amount of social security and Medicare tax to be withheld and deposited from each employee's wages. The IRS refers to rounding differences relating to employee withholding of social security and Medicare taxes as "fractions-of-cents" adjustments. If you pay your taxes with Form 941 (or Form 944) instead of making deposits because your total taxes for the quarter (year for Form 944) are less than $2,500, you also may report a fractions-of-cents adjustment.

To determine if you have a fractions-of-cents adjustment for 2016, multiply the total wages and tips for the quarter subject to:

- Social security tax reported on Form 941 or Form 944 by 6.2% (.062),

- Medicare tax reported on Form 941 or Form 944 by 1.45% (.0145), and

- Additional Medicare Tax reported on Form 941 or 944 by 0.9% (.009).

Compare these amounts (the employee share of social security and Medicare taxes) with the total social security and Medicare taxes actually withheld from employees for the quarter (from your payroll records). The difference, positive or negative, is your fractions-of-cents adjustment to be reported on Form 941, line 7, or Form 944, line 6. If the actual amount withheld is less, report a negative adjustment using a minus sign (if possible, otherwise use parentheses) in the entry space. If the actual amount is more, report a positive adjustment.

 TIP *For the above adjustments, prepare and retain a brief supporting statement explaining the nature and amount of each. Don't attach the statement to Form 941 or Form 944.*

Example. Cedar, Inc. was entitled to the following current period adjustments.

- **Fractions of cents.** Cedar, Inc. determined the amounts withheld and deposited for social security and Medicare taxes during the quarter were a net $1.44 more than the employee share of the amount figured on Form 941, lines 5a–5d, column 2 (social security and Medicare taxes). This difference was caused by adding or dropping fractions of cents when figuring social security and Medicare taxes for each wage payment. Cedar, Inc. must report a positive $1.44 fractions-of-cents adjustment on Form 941, line 7.

- **Third-party sick pay.** Cedar, Inc. included taxes of $2,000 for sick pay on Form 941, lines 5a and 5c, column 2, for social security and Medicare taxes. However, the third-party payor of the sick pay withheld and paid the employee share ($1,000) of these taxes. Cedar, Inc. is entitled to a $1,000 sick pay adjustment (negative) on Form 941, line 8.

- **Life insurance premiums.** Cedar, Inc. paid group-term life insurance premiums for policies in excess of $50,000 for former employees. The former employees must pay the employee share of the social security and Medicare taxes ($200) on the policies. However, Cedar, Inc. must include the employee share of these taxes with the social security and Medicare taxes reported on Form 941, lines 5a and 5c, column 2. Therefore, Cedar, Inc. is entitled to a negative $200 adjustment on Form 941, line 9.

Adjustment of tax on third-party sick pay. Report both the employer and employee shares of social security and Medicare taxes for sick pay on Form 941, lines 5a and 5c (Form 944, lines 4a and 4c). If the aggregate wages paid for an employee by the employer and third-party payor exceed $200,000 for the calendar year, report the Additional Medicare Tax on Form 941, line 5d (Form 944, line 4d). Show as a negative adjustment on Form 941, line 8 (Form 944, line 6), the social security and Medicare taxes withheld on sick pay by a third-party payor. See section 6 of Pub. 15-A for more information.

Adjustment of tax on tips. If, by the 10th of the month after the month you received an employee's report on tips, you don't have enough employee funds available to withhold the employee's share of social security and Medicare taxes, you no longer have to collect it. However, report the entire amount of these tips on Form 941, lines 5b and 5c (Form 944, lines 4b and 4c). If the aggregate wages and tips paid for an employee exceed $200,000 for the calendar year, report the Additional Medicare Tax on Form 941, line 5d (Form 944, line 4d). Include as a negative adjustment on Form 941, line 9 (Form 944, line 6), the total uncollected employee share of the social security and Medicare taxes.

Adjustment of tax on group-term life insurance premiums paid for former employees. The employee share of social security and Medicare taxes for premiums on group-term life insurance over $50,000 for a former employee is paid by the former employee with his or her tax return and isn't collected by the employer. However, include all social security and Medicare taxes for such coverage on Form 941, lines 5a and 5c (Form 944, lines 4a and 4c). If the amount paid for an employee for premiums on group-term life insurance combined with other wages exceeds $200,000 for the calendar year, report the Additional Medicare Tax on Form 941, line 5d (Form 944, line 4d). Back out the amount of the employee share of these taxes as a negative adjustment on Form 941, line 9 (Form 944, line 6). See Pub. 15-B for more information on group-term life insurance.

No change to record of federal tax liability. Don't make any changes to your record of federal tax liability reported on Form 941, line 14, or Schedule B (Form 941) (Form 945-A for Form 944 filers) for current period adjustments. The amounts reported on the record reflect the actual amounts you withheld from employees' wages for social security and Medicare taxes. Because the current period adjustments make the amounts reported on Form 941, lines 5a–5d, column 2 (Form 944, lines 4a–4d, column 2), equal the actual amounts you withheld (the amounts reported on the record), no additional changes to the record of federal tax liability are necessary for these adjustments.

Prior Period Adjustments

Forms for prior period adjustments. Use Form 941-X or Form 944-X to make a correction after you discover an error on a previously filed Form 941 or Form 944. There are also Forms 943-X, 945-X, and CT-1 X to report corrections on the corresponding returns. Use Form 843 when requesting a refund or abatement of assessed interest or penalties.

 TIP *See Revenue Ruling 2009-39, 2009-52 I.R.B. 951, for examples of how the interest-free adjustment and claim for refund rules apply in 10 different situations. You can find Revenue Ruling 2009-39, at www.irs.gov/irb/2009-52_IRB/ar14.html.*

Background. Treasury Decision 9405 changed the process for making interest-free adjustments to employment taxes reported on Form 941 and Form 944 and for filing a claim for refund of employment taxes. Treasury Decision 9405, 2008-32 I.R.B. 293, is available at *www.irs.gov/irb/*

_2008-32_irb/ar13.html_. You will use the adjustment process if you underreported employment taxes and are making a payment, or if you overreported employment taxes and will be applying the credit to the Form 941 or Form 944 period during which you file Form 941-X or Form 944-X. You will use the claim process if you overreported employment taxes and are requesting a refund or abatement of the overreported amount. We use the terms "correct" and "corrections" to include interest-free adjustments under sections 6205 and 6413, and claims for refund and abatement under sections 6402, 6414, and 6404 of the Internal Revenue Code.

Correcting employment taxes. When you discover an error on a previously filed Form 941 or Form 944, you must:

- Correct that error using Form 941-X or Form 944-X,

- File a separate Form 941-X or Form 944-X for each Form 941 or Form 944 you are correcting, and

- File Form 941-X or Form 944-X separately. Don't file with Form 941 or Form 944.

Continue to report current quarter adjustments for fractions of cents, third-party sick pay, tips, and group-term life insurance on Form 941 using lines 7–9, and on Form 944 using line 6.

Report the correction of underreported and overreported amounts for the same tax period on a single Form 941-X or Form 944-X unless you are requesting a refund. If you are requesting a refund and are correcting both underreported and overreported amounts, file one Form 941-X or Form 944-X correcting the underreported amounts only and a second Form 941-X or Form 944-X correcting the overreported amounts.

See the chart on the back of Form 941-X or Form 944-X for help in choosing whether to use the adjustment process or the claim process. See the Instructions for Form 941-X or the Instructions for Form 944-X for details on how to make the adjustment or claim for refund or abatement.

Income tax withholding adjustments. In a current calendar year, correct prior quarter income tax withholding errors by making the correction on Form 941-X when you discover the error.

You may make an adjustment only to correct income tax withholding errors discovered during the same calendar year in which you paid the wages. This is because the employee uses the amount shown on Form W-2 as a credit when filing his or her income tax return (Form 1040, etc.).

You can't adjust amounts reported as income tax withheld in a prior calendar year unless it is to correct an administrative error or IRC section 3509 applies. An administrative error occurs if the amount you entered on Form 941 or Form 944 isn't the amount you actually withheld. For example, if the total income tax actually withheld was incorrectly reported on Form 941 or Form 944 due to a mathematical or transposition error, this would be an administrative error. The administrative error adjustment corrects the amount reported on Form 941 or Form 944 to agree with the amount actually withheld from employees and reported on their Forms W-2.

Additional Medicare Tax withholding adjustments. Generally, the rules discussed above under _Income tax withholding adjustments_ apply to Additional Medicare Tax withholding adjustments. That is, you may make an adjustment to correct Additional Medicare Tax withholding errors discovered during the same calendar year in which you paid wages. You can't adjust amounts reported in a prior calendar year unless it is to correct an administrative error or IRC section 3509 applies. If you have overpaid Additional Medicare Tax, you can't file a claim for refund for the amount of the overpayment unless the amount wasn't actually withheld from the employee's wages (which would be an administrative error).

If a prior year error was a nonadministrative error, you may correct only the **wages and tips** subject to Additional Medicare Tax withholding.

Collecting underwithheld taxes from employees. If you withheld no income, social security, or Medicare taxes or less than the correct amount from an employee's wages, you can make it up from later pay to that employee. But you are the one who owes the underpayment. Reimbursement is a matter for settlement between you and the employee. Underwithheld income tax and Additional Medicare Tax must be recovered from the employee on or before the last day of the calendar year. There are special rules for tax on tips (see section 6) and fringe benefits (see section 5).

Refunding amounts incorrectly withheld from employees. If you withheld more than the correct amount of income, social security, or Medicare taxes from wages paid, repay or reimburse the employee the excess. Any excess income tax or Additional Medicare Tax withholding must be repaid or reimbursed to the employee before the end of the calendar year in which it was withheld. Keep in your records the employee's written receipt showing the date and amount of the repayment or record of reimbursement. If you didn't repay or reimburse the employee, you must report and pay each excess amount when you file Form 941 for the quarter (or Form 944 for the year) in which you withheld too much tax.

Correcting filed Forms W-2 and W-3. When adjustments are made to correct wages and social security and Medicare taxes because of a change in the wage totals reported for a previous year, you also need to file Form W-2c and Form W-3c with the SSA. Up to 25 Forms W-2c per Form W-3c may now be filed per session over the Internet, with no limit on the number of sessions. For more information, visit the Social Security Administration's Employer W-2 Filing Instructions & Information webpage at _www.socialsecurity.gov/employer_.

Exceptions to interest-free corrections of employment taxes. A correction won't be eligible for interest-free treatment if:

- The failure to report relates to an issue raised in an IRS examination of a prior return, or

- The employer knowingly underreported its employment tax liability.

A correction won't be eligible for interest-free treatment after the earlier of the following:

- Receipt of an IRS notice and demand for payment after assessment or
- Receipt of an IRS Notice of Determination of Worker Classification (Letter 3523).

Wage Repayments

If an employee repays you for wages received in error, don't offset the repayments against current-year wages unless the repayments are for amounts received in error in the current year.

Repayment of current year wages. If you receive repayments for wages paid during a prior quarter in the current year, report adjustments on Form 941-X to recover income tax withholding and social security and Medicare taxes for the repaid wages.

Repayment of prior year wages. If you receive repayments for wages paid during a prior year, report an adjustment on Form 941-X or Form 944-X to recover the social security and Medicare taxes. You can't make an adjustment for income tax withholding because the wages were income to the employee for the prior year. You can't make an adjustment for Additional Medicare Tax withholding because the employee determines liability for Additional Medicare Tax on the employee's income tax return for the prior year.

You also must file Forms W-2c and W-3c with the SSA to correct social security and Medicare wages and taxes. Don't correct wages (box 1) on Form W-2c for the amount paid in error. Give a copy of Form W-2c to the employee.

Employee reporting of repayment. The wages paid in error in the prior year remain taxable to the employee for that year. This is because the employee received and had use of those funds during that year. The employee isn't entitled to file an amended return (Form 1040X) to recover the income tax on these wages. Instead, the employee is entitled to a deduction (or credit in some cases) for the repaid wages on his or her income tax return for the year of repayment. However, the employee should file an amended return (Form 1040X) to recover any Additional Medicare Tax paid on the wages paid in error in the prior year.

14. Federal Unemployment (FUTA) Tax

The Federal Unemployment Tax Act, with state unemployment systems, provides for payments of unemployment compensation to workers who have lost their jobs. Most employers pay both a federal and a state unemployment tax. For a list of state unemployment agencies, visit the U.S. Department of Labor's website at *www.workforcesecurity.doleta.gov/unemploy/agencies.asp.* Only the employer pays FUTA tax; it isn't withheld from the employee's wages. For more information, see the Instructions for Form 940.

 Services rendered to a federally recognized Indian tribal government (or any subdivision, subsidiary, or business wholly owned by such an Indian tribe) are exempt from FUTA tax, subject to the tribe's compliance with state law. For more information, see Internal Revenue Code section 3309(d).

Who must pay? Use the following three tests to determine whether you must pay FUTA tax. Each test applies to a different category of employee, and each is independent of the others. If a test describes your situation, you are subject to FUTA tax on the wages you pay to employees in that category during the current calendar year.

1. **General test.**
   You are subject to FUTA tax in 2016 on the wages you pay employees who aren't farmworkers or household workers if:

   a. You paid wages of $1,500 or more in any calendar quarter in 2015 or 2016, or

   b. You had one or more employees for at least some part of a day in any 20 or more different weeks in 2015 or 20 or more different weeks in 2016.

2. **Household employees test.**
   You are subject to FUTA tax if you paid total cash wages of $1,000 or more to household employees in any calendar quarter in 2015 or 2016. A household employee is an employee who performs household work in a private home, local college club, or local fraternity or sorority chapter.

3. **Farmworkers test.**
   You are subject to FUTA tax on the wages you pay to farmworkers if:

   a. You paid cash wages of $20,000 or more to farmworkers during any calendar quarter in 2015 or 2016, or

   b. You employed 10 or more farmworkers during at least some part of a day (whether or not at the same time) during any 20 or more different weeks in 2015 or 20 or more different weeks in 2016.

Computing FUTA tax. For 2016, the FUTA tax rate is 6.0%. The tax applies to the first $7,000 you pay to each employee as wages during the year. The $7,000 is the federal wage base. Your state wage base may be different.

Generally, you can take a credit against your FUTA tax for amounts you paid into state unemployment funds. The credit may be as much as 5.4% of FUTA taxable wages. If you are entitled to the maximum 5.4% credit, the FUTA tax rate after credit is 0.6%. You are entitled to the maximum credit if you paid your state unemployment taxes in full, on time, and on all the same wages as are subject to FUTA tax, and as long as the state isn't determined to be a credit reduction state. See the Instructions for Form 940 to determine the credit.

In some states, the wages subject to state unemployment tax are the same as the wages subject to FUTA tax. However, certain states exclude some types of wages from state unemployment tax, even though they are subject to FUTA tax (for example, wages paid to corporate officers, certain payments of sick pay by unions, and certain fringe benefits). In such a case, you may be required to deposit more than 0.6% FUTA tax on those wages. See the Instructions for Form 940 for further guidance.

 In years when there are credit reduction states, you must include liabilities owed for credit reduction with your fourth quarter deposit. You may deposit the anticipated extra liability throughout the year, but it isn't due until the due date for the deposit for the fourth quarter, and the associated liability should be recorded as being incurred in the fourth quarter. See the Instructions for Form 940 for more information.

Successor employer. If you acquired a business from an employer who was liable for FUTA tax, you may be able to count the wages that employer paid to the employees who continue to work for you when you figure the $7,000 FUTA tax wage base. See the Instructions for Form 940.

Depositing FUTA tax. For deposit purposes, figure FUTA tax quarterly. Determine your FUTA tax liability by multiplying the amount of taxable wages paid during the quarter by 0.6%. Stop depositing FUTA tax on an employee's wages when he or she reaches $7,000 in taxable wages for the calendar year.

If your FUTA tax liability for any calendar quarter is $500 or less, you don't have to deposit the tax. Instead, you may carry it forward and add it to the liability figured in the next quarter to see if you must make a deposit. If your FUTA tax liability for any calendar quarter is over $500 (including any FUTA tax carried forward from an earlier quarter), you must deposit the tax by EFT. See section 11 for more information on EFT.

Household employees. You aren't required to deposit FUTA taxes for household employees unless you report their wages on Form 941, 943, or 944. See Pub. 926 for more information.

When to deposit. Deposit the FUTA tax by the last day of the first month that follows the end of the quarter. If the due date for making your deposit falls on a Saturday, Sunday, or legal holiday, you may make your deposit on the next business day. See *Legal holiday*, earlier, for a list of the legal holidays for 2016.

If your liability for the fourth quarter (plus any undeposited amount from any earlier quarter) is over $500, deposit the entire amount by the due date of Form 940 (January 31). If it is $500 or less, you can make a deposit, pay the tax with a credit or debit card, or pay the tax with your 2015 Form 940 by February 1, 2016. If you file Form 940 electronically, you can e-file and e-pay (EFW). For more information on paying your taxes with a credit or debit card or using EFW, visit the IRS website at *www.irs.gov/payments*.

Table 4. **When to Deposit FUTA Taxes**

Quarter	Ending	Due Date
Jan.–Feb.–Mar.	Mar. 31	Apr. 30
Apr.–May–June	June 30	July 31
July–Aug.–Sept.	Sept. 30	Oct. 31
Oct.–Nov.–Dec.	Dec. 31	Jan. 31

Reporting FUTA tax. Use Form 940 to report FUTA tax. File your 2015 Form 940 by February 1, 2016. However, if you deposited all FUTA tax when due, you may file on or before February 10, 2016.

Form 940 e-file. The Form 940 e-file program allows a taxpayer to electronically file From 940 using a computer with an internet connection and commercial tax preparation software. For more information, visit the IRS website at *www.irs.gov/efile*, or call 1-866-255-0654.

Household employees. If you didn't report employment taxes for household employees on Forms 941, 943, or 944, report FUTA tax for these employees on Schedule H (Form 1040). See Pub. 926 for more information. You must have an EIN to file Schedule H (Form 1040).

Electronic filing by reporting agents. Reporting agents filing Forms 940 for groups of taxpayers can file them electronically. See the *Reporting Agent* discussion in section 7 of Pub. 15-A.

15. Special Rules for Various Types of Services and Payments

Section references are to the Internal Revenue Code unless otherwise noted.

Special Classes of Employment and Special Types of Payments	Treatment Under Employment Taxes		
	Income Tax Withholding	Social Security and Medicare (including Additional Medicare Tax when wages are paid in excess of $200,000)	FUTA
Aliens, nonresident.	See Pub. 515 and Pub. 519.		
Aliens, resident:			
1. Service performed in the U.S.	Same as U.S. citizen.	Same as U.S. citizen. (Exempt if any part of service as crew member of foreign vessel or aircraft is performed outside U.S.)	Same as U.S. citizen.
2. Service performed outside U.S.	Withhold	Taxable if (1) working for an American employer or (2) an American employer by agreement covers U.S. citizens and residents employed by its foreign affiliates.	Exempt unless on or in connection with an American vessel or aircraft and either performed under contract made in U.S., or alien is employed on such vessel or aircraft when it touches U.S. port.
Cafeteria plan benefits under section 125.	If employee chooses cash, subject to all employment taxes. If employee chooses another benefit, the treatment is the same as if the benefit was provided outside the plan. See Pub. 15-B for more information.		
Deceased worker:			
1. Wages paid to beneficiary or estate in same calendar year as worker's death. See the Instructions for Forms W-2 and W-3 for details.	Exempt	Taxable	Taxable
2. Wages paid to beneficiary or estate after calendar year of worker's death.	Exempt	Exempt	Exempt
Dependent care assistance programs.	Exempt to the extent it is reasonable to believe amounts are excludable from gross income under section 129.		
Disabled worker's wages paid after year in which worker became entitled to disability insurance benefits under the Social Security Act.	Withhold	Exempt, if worker didn't perform any service for employer during period for which payment is made.	Taxable
Employee business expense reimbursement:			
1. Accountable plan.			
a. Amounts not exceeding specified government rate for per diem or standard mileage.	Exempt	Exempt	Exempt
b. Amounts in excess of specified government rate for per diem or standard mileage.	Withhold	Taxable	Taxable
2. Nonaccountable plan. See section 5 for details.	Withhold	Taxable	Taxable
Family employees:			
1. Child employed by parent (or partnership in which each partner is a parent of the child).	Withhold	Exempt until age 18; age 21 for domestic service.	Exempt until age 21
2. Parent employed by child.	Withhold	Taxable if in course of the son's or daughter's business. For domestic services, see section 3.	Exempt
3. Spouse employed by spouse. See section 3 for more information.	Withhold	Taxable if in course of spouse's business.	Exempt
Fishing and related activities.	See Pub. 334.		
Foreign governments and international organizations.	Exempt	Exempt	Exempt

Special Classes of Employment and Special Types of Payments	Treatment Under Employment Taxes		
	Income Tax Withholding	Social Security and Medicare (including Additional Medicare Tax when wages are paid in excess of $200,000)	FUTA
Foreign service by U.S. citizens:			
1. As U.S. government employees.	Withhold	Same as within U.S.	Exempt
2. For foreign affiliates of American employers and other private employers.	Exempt if at time of payment (1) it is reasonable to believe employee is entitled to exclusion from income under section 911 or (2) the employer is required by law of the foreign country to withhold income tax on such payment.	Exempt unless (1) an American employer by agreement covers U.S. citizens employed by its foreign affiliates or (2) U.S. citizen works for American employer.	Exempt unless (1) on American vessel or aircraft and work is performed under contract made in U.S. or worker is employed on vessel when it touches U.S. port or (2) U.S. citizen works for American employer (except in a contiguous country with which the U.S. has an agreement for unemployment compensation) or in the U.S. Virgin Islands.
Fringe benefits.	Taxable on excess of fair market value of the benefit over the sum of an amount paid for it by the employee and any amount excludable by law. However, special valuation rules may apply. Benefits provided under cafeteria plans may qualify for exclusion from wages for social security, Medicare, and FUTA taxes. See Pub. 15-B for details.		
Government employment: State/local governments and political subdivisions, employees of:			
1. Salaries and wages (includes payments to most elected and appointed officials.) See chapter 3 of Pub. 963.	Withhold	Generally, taxable for (1) services performed by employees who are either (a) covered under a section 218 agreement or (b) not covered under a section 218 agreement and not a member of a public retirement system (mandatory social security and Medicare coverage), and (2) (for Medicare tax only) for services performed by employees hired or rehired after 3/31/86 who aren't covered under a section 218 agreement or the mandatory social security provisions, unless specifically excluded by law. See Pub. 963.	Exempt
2. Election workers. Election individuals are workers who are employed to perform services for state or local governments at election booths in connection with national, state, or local elections. **Note:** File Form W-2 for payments of $600 or more even if no social security, or Medicare taxes were withheld.	Exempt	Taxable if paid $1,700 or more in 2016 (lesser amount if specified by a section 218 social security agreement). See Revenue Ruling 2000-6.	Exempt
3. Emergency workers. Emergency workers who were hired on a temporary basis in response to a specific unforeseen emergency and aren't intended to become permanent employees.	Withhold	Exempt if serving on a temporary basis in case of fire, storm, snow, earthquake, flood, or similar emergency.	Exempt
U.S. federal government employees.	Withhold	Taxable for Medicare. Taxable for social security unless hired before 1984. See section 3121(b)(5).	Exempt

Special Classes of Employment and Special Types of Payments	Treatment Under Employment Taxes		
	Income Tax Withholding	**Social Security and Medicare (including Additional Medicare Tax when wages are paid in excess of $200,000)**	**FUTA**
Homeworkers (industrial, cottage industry):			
1. Common law employees.	Withhold	Taxable	Taxable
2. Statutory employees. See section 2 for details.	Exempt	Taxable if paid $100 or more in cash in a year.	Exempt
Hospital employees:			
1. Interns.	Withhold	Taxable	Exempt
2. Patients.	Withhold	Taxable (Exempt for state or local government hospitals.)	Exempt
Household employees:			
1. Domestic service in private homes. Farmers, see Pub. 51.	Exempt (withhold if both employer and employee agree).	Taxable if paid $2,000 or more in cash in 2016. Exempt if performed by an individual under age 18 during any portion of the calendar year and isn't the principal occupation of the employee.	Taxable if employer paid total cash wages of $1,000 or more in any quarter in the current or preceding calendar year.
2. Domestic service in college clubs, fraternities, and sororities.	Exempt (withhold if both employer and employee agree).	Exempt if paid to regular student; also exempt if employee is paid less than $100 in a year by an income-tax-exempt employer.	Taxable if employer paid total cash wages of $1,000 or more in any quarter in the current or preceding calendar year.
Insurance for employees:			
1. Accident and health insurance premiums under a plan or system for employees and their dependents generally or for a class or classes of employees and their dependents.	Exempt (except 2% shareholder-employees of S corporations).	Exempt	Exempt
2. Group-term life insurance costs. See Pub. 15-B for details	Exempt	Exempt, except for the cost of group-term life insurance includible in the employee's gross income. Special rules apply for former employees.	Exempt
Insurance agents or solicitors:			
1. Full-time life insurance salesperson.	Withhold only if employee under common law. See section 2.	Taxable	Taxable if (1) employee under common law and (2) not paid solely by commissions.
2. Other salesperson of life, casualty, etc., insurance.	Withhold only if employee under common law.	Taxable only if employee under common law.	Taxable if (1) employee under common law and (2) not paid solely by commissions.
Interest on loans with below-market interest rates (foregone interest and deemed original issue discount).	See Pub. 15-A.		
Leave-sharing plans: Amounts paid to an employee under a leave-sharing plan.	Withhold	Taxable	Taxable
Newspaper carriers and vendors: Newspaper carriers under age 18; newspaper and magazine vendors buying at fixed prices and retaining receipts from sales to customers. See Pub. 15-A for information on statutory nonemployee status.	Exempt (withhold if both employer and employee voluntarily agree).	Exempt	Exempt

Special Classes of Employment and Special Types of Payments	Treatment Under Employment Taxes		
	Income Tax Withholding	Social Security and Medicare (including Additional Medicare Tax when wages are paid in excess of $200,000)	FUTA
Noncash payments:			
1. For household work, agricultural labor, and service not in the course of the employer's trade or business.	Exempt (withhold if both employer and employee voluntarily agree).	Exempt	Exempt
2. To certain retail commission salespersons ordinarily paid solely on a cash commission basis.	Optional with employer, except to the extent employee's supplemental wages during the year exceed $1 million.	Taxable	Taxable
Nonprofit organizations.	See Pub. 15-A.		
Officers or shareholders of an S Corporation: Distributions and other payments by an S corporation to a corporate officer or shareholder must be treated as wages to the extent the amounts are reasonable compensation for services to the corporation by an employee. See the Instructions for Form 1120S.	Withhold	Taxable	Taxable
Partners: Payments to general or limited partners of a partnership. See Pub. 541 for partner reporting rules.	Exempt	Exempt	Exempt
Railroads: Payments subject to the Railroad Retirement Act. See Pub. 915 for more details.	Withhold	Exempt	Exempt
Religious exemptions.	See Pub. 15-A and Pub. 517.		
Retirement and pension plans:			
1. Employer contributions to a qualified plan.	Exempt	Exempt	Exempt
2. Elective employee contributions and deferrals to a plan containing a qualified cash or deferred compensation arrangement (for example, 401(k)).	Generally exempt, but see section 402(g) for limitation.	Taxable	Taxable
3. Employer contributions to individual retirement accounts under simplified employee pension plan (SEP).	Generally exempt, but see section 402(g) for salary reduction SEP limitation.	Exempt, except for amounts contributed under a salary reduction SEP agreement.	
4. Employer contributions to section 403(b) annuities.	Generally exempt, but see section 402(g) for limitation.	Taxable if paid through a salary reduction agreement (written or otherwise).	
5. Employee salary reduction contributions to a SIMPLE retirement account.	Exempt	Taxable	Taxable
6. Distributions from qualified retirement and pension plans and section 403(b) annuities. See Pub. 15-A for information on pensions, annuities, and employer contributions to nonqualified deferred compensation arrangements.	Withhold, but recipient may elect exemption on Form W-4P in certain cases; mandatory 20% withholding applies to an eligible rollover distribution that isn't a direct rollover; exempt for direct rollover. See Pub. 15-A.	Exempt	Exempt
7. Employer contributions to a section 457(b) plan.	Generally exempt but see section 402(g) limitation.	Taxable	Taxable
8. Employee salary reduction contributions to a section 457(b) plan.	Generally exempt but see section 402(g) salary reduction limitation.	Taxable	Taxable
Salespersons:			
1. Common law employees.	Withhold	Taxable	Taxable
2. Statutory employees.	Exempt	Taxable	Taxable, except for full-time life insurance sales agents.
3. Statutory nonemployees (qualified real estate agents, direct sellers, and certain companion sitters). See Pub. 15-A for details.	Exempt	Exempt	Exempt

Special Classes of Employment and Special Types of Payments	Treatment Under Employment Taxes		
	Income Tax Withholding	Social Security and Medicare (including Additional Medicare Tax when wages are paid in excess of $200,000)	FUTA
Scholarships and fellowship grants (includible in income under section 117(c)).	Withhold	Taxability depends on the nature of the employment and the status of the organization. See *Students, scholars, trainees, teachers, etc.* below.	
Severance or dismissal pay.	Withhold	Taxable	Taxable
Service not in the course of the employer's trade or business (other than on a farm operated for profit or for household employment in private homes).	Withhold only if employee earns $50 or more in cash in a quarter and works on 24 or more different days in that quarter or in the preceding quarter.	Taxable if employee receives $100 or more in cash in a calendar year.	Taxable only if employee earns $50 or more in cash in a quarter and works on 24 or more different days in that quarter or in the preceding quarter.
Sick pay. See Pub. 15-A for more information.	Withhold	Exempt after end of 6 calendar months after the calendar month employee last worked for employer.	
Students, scholars, trainees, teachers, etc.:			
1. Student enrolled and regularly attending classes, performing services for:			
a. Private school, college, or university.	Withhold	Exempt	Exempt
b. Auxiliary nonprofit organization operated for and controlled by school, college, or university.	Withhold	Exempt unless services are covered by a section 218 (Social Security Act) agreement.	Exempt
c. Public school, college, or university.	Withhold	Exempt unless services are covered by a section 218 (Social Security Act) agreement.	Exempt
2. Full-time student performing service for academic credit, combining instruction with work experience as an integral part of the program.	Withhold	Taxable	Exempt unless program was established for or on behalf of an employer or group of employers.
3. Student nurse performing part-time services for nominal earnings at hospital as incidental part of training.	Withhold	Exempt	Exempt
4. Student employed by organized camps.	Withhold	Taxable	Exempt
5. Student, scholar, trainee, teacher, etc., as nonimmigrant alien under section 101(a)(15)(F), (J), (M), or (Q) of Immigration and Nationality Act (that is, aliens holding F-1, J-1, M-1, or Q-1 visas).	Withhold unless excepted by regulations.	Exempt if service is performed for purpose specified in section 101(a)(15)(F), (J), (M), or (Q) of Immigration and Nationality Act. However, these taxes may apply if the employee becomes a resident alien. See the special residency tests for exempt individuals in chapter 1 of Pub. 519.	
Supplemental unemployment compensation plan benefits.	Withhold	Exempt under certain conditions. See Pub. 15-A.	
Tips:			
1. If $20 or more in a month.	Withhold	Taxable	Taxable for all tips reported in writing to employer.
2. If less than $20 in a month. See section 6 for more information.	Exempt	Exempt	Exempt
Worker's compensation.	Exempt	Exempt	Exempt

16. Third Party Payer Arrangements

An employer may outsource some or all of its federal employment tax withholding, reporting and payment obligations. An employer who outsources payroll and related tax duties (that is, withholding, reporting, and paying over social security, Medicare, FUTA, and income taxes) to a third party payer, generally will remain responsible for those duties, including liability for the taxes.

If an employer outsources some or all of its payroll responsibilities, the employer should consider the following information.

- The employer remains responsible for federal tax deposits and other federal tax payments even though the employer may forward the tax amounts to the third party payer to make the deposits and payments. If the third party fails to make the deposits and payments, the IRS may assess penalties and interest on the employer's account. As the employer, you may be liable for all taxes, penalties, and interest due. The employer may also be held personally liable for certain unpaid federal taxes.

- If the employer's account has any issues, the IRS will send correspondence to the employer at the address of record. We strongly recommend that the employer maintain its address as the address of record with the IRS. Having correspondence sent to the address of the third party payer may significantly limit the employer's ability to be informed about tax matters involving the employer's business.

The following are common third party payers who an employer may contract with to perform payroll and related tax duties.

- Payroll service provider (PSP).

- Reporting agent.

- Agent with approved Form 2678.

- Payer designated under section 3504.

Payroll service provider (PSP). A PSP helps administer payroll and payroll related tax duties on behalf of the employer. A PSP may prepare paychecks for employees, prepare and file employment tax returns, prepare Form W-2, and make federal tax deposits and other federal tax payments. A PSP performs these functions using the EIN of the employer. A PSP isn't liable as either an employer or an agent of the employer for the employer's employment taxes. If an employer is using a PSP to perform its tax duties, the employer remains liable for its employment tax obligations, including liability for employment taxes.

An employer who uses a PSP should ensure the PSP is using EFTPS to make federal tax deposits on behalf of the employer so the employer can confirm that the payments are being made on its behalf.

Reporting agent. A reporting agent is a type of PSP. A reporting agent helps administer payroll and payroll related tax duties on behalf of the employer, including authorization to electronically sign and file forms set forth on Form 8655. An employer uses Form 8655 to authorize a reporting agent to perform functions on behalf of the employer. A reporting agent performs these functions using the EIN of the employer. A reporting agent isn't liable as either an employer or an agent of the employer for the employer's employment taxes. If an employer is using a reporting agent to perform its tax duties, the employer remains liable for its employment obligations, including liability for employment taxes.

A reporting agent must use EFTPS to make federal tax deposits on behalf of an employer. The employer has access to EFTPS to confirm federal tax deposits were made on its behalf.

For more information on reporting agents, see Revenue Procedure 2012-32, 2012-34 I.R.B. 267, at *www.irs.gov/irb/2012-34_IRB/ar08.html* and Pub. 1474, Technical Specifications Guide for Reporting Agent Authorization and Federal Tax Depositors.

Agent with an approved Form 2678. An agent with an approved Form 2678 helps administer payroll and related tax duties on behalf of the employer. An agent authorized under section 3504 may pay wages or compensation to some or all of the employees of an employer, prepare and file employment tax returns as set forth on Form 2678, prepare Form W-2, and make federal tax deposits and other federal tax payments. An employer uses Form 2678 to request authorization to appoint an agent to perform functions on behalf of the employer. An agent with an approved Form 2678 is authorized to perform these functions using its own EIN. The agent files a Schedule R (Form 941) to allocate wages and taxes to the employers it represents as an agent.

If an employer is using an agent with an approved Form 2678 to perform its tax duties, the agent and the employer are jointly liable for the employment taxes and related tax duties for which the agent is authorized to perform.

Form 2678 doesn't apply to FUTA taxes reportable on Form 940 unless the employer is a home care service recipient receiving home care services through a program administered by a federal, state, or local government agency.

For more information on an agent with an approved Form 2678, see Revenue Procedure 2013-39, 2013-52 I.R.B. 830, at *www.irs.gov/irb/2013-52_IRB/ar15.html*.

Payer designated under section 3504. In certain circumstances, the IRS may designate a third party payer to perform the acts of an employer. The IRS will designate a third party payer on behalf of an employer if the third party has a service agreement with the employer. A service agreement is an agreement between the third party payer and an employer in which the third party payer (1) asserts it is the employer of individuals performing services for the employer; (2) pays wages to the individuals that perform services for the employer; and (3) assumes responsibility to withhold, report, and pay federal employment taxes for the wages it pays to the individuals that perform services for the employer.

A payer designated under section 3504 performs tax duties under the service agreement using its own EIN. If the IRS designates a third party payer under section 3504, the designated payer and the employer are jointly liable for the employment taxes and related tax duties for which the third party payer is designated.

For more information on a payer designated under section 3504, see Regulations section 31.3504-2.

17. How To Use the Income Tax Withholding Tables

There are several ways to figure income tax withholding. The following methods of withholding are based on the information you get from your employees on Form W-4. See section 9 for more information on Form W-4.

 Adjustments aren't required when there will be more than the usual number of pay periods, for example, 27 biweekly pay dates instead of 26.

Wage Bracket Method

Under the wage bracket method, find the proper table (on pages 46–65) for your payroll period and the employee's marital status as shown on his or her Form W-4. Then, based on the number of withholding allowances claimed on the Form W-4 and the amount of wages, find the amount of income tax to withhold. If your employee is claiming more than 10 withholding allowances, see below.

If you can't use the wage bracket tables because wages exceed the amount shown in the last bracket of the table, use the percentage method of withholding described below. Be sure to reduce wages by the amount of total withholding allowances in *Table 5* before using the percentage method tables (pages 44–45).

Adjusting wage bracket withholding for employees claiming more than 10 withholding allowances. The wage bracket tables can be used if an employee claims up to 10 allowances. More than 10 allowances may be claimed because of the special withholding allowance, additional allowances for deductions and credits, and the system itself.

Adapt the tables to more than 10 allowances as follows:

1. Multiply the number of withholding allowances over 10 by the allowance value for the payroll period. The allowance values are in *Table 5* below.

2. Subtract the result from the employee's wages.

3. On this amount, find and withhold the tax in the column for 10 allowances.

This is a voluntary method. If you use the wage bracket tables, you may continue to withhold the amount in the

"10" column when your employee has more than 10 allowances, using the method above. You can also use any other method described next.

Percentage Method

If you don't want to use the wage bracket tables on pages 46–65 to figure how much income tax to withhold, you can use a percentage computation based on *Table 5* below and the appropriate rate table. This method works for any number of withholding allowances the employee claims and any amount of wages.

Use these steps to figure the income tax to withhold under the percentage method.

1. Multiply one withholding allowance for your payroll period (see *Table 5* below) by the number of allowances the employee claims.

2. Subtract that amount from the employee's wages.

3. Determine the amount to withhold from the appropriate table on pages 44–45.

Table 5. **Percentage Method—2016 Amount for One Withholding Allowance**

Payroll Period	One Withholding Allowance
Weekly	$ 77.90
Biweekly	155.80
Semimonthly	168.80
Monthly	337.50
Quarterly	1,012.50
Semiannually	2,025.00
Annually	4,050.00
Daily or miscellaneous (each day of the payroll period)	15.60

Example. An unmarried employee is paid $800 weekly. This employee has in effect a Form W-4 claiming two withholding allowances. Using the percentage method, figure the income tax to withhold as follows:

1.	Total wage payment		$800.00
2.	One allowance	$77.90	
3.	Allowances claimed on Form W-4 . .	2	
4.	Multiply line 2 by line 3		$155.80
5	Amount subject to withholding (subtract line 4 from line 1)		$644.20
6.	Tax to be withheld on $644.20 from Table 1—single person, page 44 . . .		$81.23

To figure the income tax to withhold, you may reduce the last digit of the wages to zero, or figure the wages to the nearest dollar.

Annual income tax withholding. Figure the income tax to withhold on annual wages under the *Percentage Method* for an annual payroll period. Then prorate the tax back to the payroll period.

Example. A married person claims four withholding allowances. She is paid $1,000 a week. Multiply the weekly wages by 52 weeks to figure the annual wage of $52,000. Subtract $16,200 (the value of four withholding allowances for 2016) for a balance of $35,800. Using the table for the annual payroll period on page 45, $3,160.00 is withheld. Divide the annual tax by 52. The weekly income tax to withhold is $60.77.

Alternative Methods of Income Tax Withholding

Rather than the *Wage Bracket Method* or *Percentage Method* described in this section, you can use an alternative method to withhold income tax. Pub. 15-A describes these alternative methods and contains:

- Formula tables for percentage method withholding (for automated payroll systems),

- Wage bracket percentage method tables (for automated payroll systems), and

- Combined income, social security, and Medicare tax withholding tables.

Some of the alternative methods explained in Pub. 15-A are annualized wages, average estimated wages, cumulative wages, and part-year employment.

Percentage Method Tables for Income Tax Withholding

(For Wages Paid in 2016)

TABLE 1—WEEKLY Payroll Period

(a) SINGLE person (including head of household)—

If the amount of wages (after subtracting withholding allowances) is:
Not over $43 . . . . The amount of income tax to withhold is: $0

Over—	But not over—		of excess over—
$43	—$222 . .	$0.00 plus 10%	—$43
$222	—$767 . .	$17.90 plus 15%	—$222
$767	—$1,796 . .	$99.65 plus 25%	—$767
$1,796	—$3,700 . .	$356.90 plus 28%	—$1,796
$3,700	—$7,992 . .	$890.02 plus 33%	—$3,700
$7,992	—$8,025 . .	$2,306.38 plus 35%	—$7,992
$8,025	. . . .	$2,317.93 plus 39.6%	—$8,025

(b) MARRIED person—

If the amount of wages (after subtracting withholding allowances) is:
Not over $164 . . . . The amount of income tax to withhold is: $0

Over—	But not over—		of excess over—
$164	—$521 . .	$0.00 plus 10%	—$164
$521	—$1,613 . .	$35.70 plus 15%	—$521
$1,613	—$3,086 . .	$199.50 plus 25%	—$1,613
$3,086	—$4,615 . .	$567.75 plus 28%	—$3,086
$4,615	—$8,113 . .	$995.87 plus 33%	—$4,615
$8,113	—$9,144 . .	$2,150.21 plus 35%	—$8,113
$9,144	. . . .	$2,511.06 plus 39.6%	—$9,144

TABLE 2—BIWEEKLY Payroll Period

(a) SINGLE person (including head of household)—

If the amount of wages (after subtracting withholding allowances) is:
Not over $87 . . . . The amount of income tax to withhold is: $0

Over—	But not over—		of excess over—
$87	—$443 . .	$0.00 plus 10%	—$87
$443	—$1,535 . .	$35.60 plus 15%	—$443
$1,535	—$3,592 . .	$199.40 plus 25%	—$1,535
$3,592	—$7,400 . .	$713.65 plus 28%	—$3,592
$7,400	—$15,985 . .	$1,779.89 plus 33%	—$7,400
$15,985	—$16,050 . .	$4,612.94 plus 35%	—$15,985
$16,050	. . . .	$4,635.69 plus 39.6%	—$16,050

(b) MARRIED person—

If the amount of wages (after subtracting withholding allowances) is:
Not over $329 . . . . The amount of income tax to withhold is: $0

Over—	But not over—		of excess over—
$329	—$1,042 . .	$0.00 plus 10%	—$329
$1,042	—$3,225 . .	$71.30 plus 15%	—$1,042
$3,225	—$6,171 . .	$398.75 plus 25%	—$3,225
$6,171	—$9,231 . .	$1,135.25 plus 28%	—$6,171
$9,231	—$16,227 . .	$1,992.05 plus 33%	—$9,231
$16,227	—$18,288 . .	$4,300.73 plus 35%	—$16,227
$18,288	. . . .	$5,022.08 plus 39.6%	—$18,288

TABLE 3—SEMIMONTHLY Payroll Period

(a) SINGLE person (including head of household)—

If the amount of wages (after subtracting withholding allowances) is:
Not over $94 . . . . The amount of income tax to withhold is: $0

Over—	But not over—		of excess over—
$94	—$480 . .	$0.00 plus 10%	—$94
$480	—$1,663 . .	$38.60 plus 15%	—$480
$1,663	—$3,892 . .	$216.05 plus 25%	—$1,663
$3,892	—$8,017 . .	$773.30 plus 28%	—$3,892
$8,017	—$17,317 . .	$1,928.30 plus 33%	—$8,017
$17,317	—$17,388 . .	$4,997.30 plus 35%	—$17,317
$17,388	. . . .	$5,022.15 plus 39.6%	—$17,388

(b) MARRIED person—

If the amount of wages (after subtracting withholding allowances) is:
Not over $356 . . . . The amount of income tax to withhold is: $0

Over—	But not over—		of excess over—
$356	—$1,129 . .	$0.00 plus 10%	—$356
$1,129	—$3,494 . .	$77.30 plus 15%	—$1,129
$3,494	—$6,685 . .	$432.05 plus 25%	—$3,494
$6,685	—$10,000 . .	$1,229.80 plus 28%	—$6,685
$10,000	—$17,579 . .	$2,158.00 plus 33%	—$10,000
$17,579	—$19,813 . .	$4,659.07 plus 35%	—$17,579
$19,813	. . . .	$5,440.97 plus 39.6%	—$19,813

TABLE 4—MONTHLY Payroll Period

(a) SINGLE person (including head of household)—

If the amount of wages (after subtracting withholding allowances) is:
Not over $188 . . . . The amount of income tax to withhold is: $0

Over—	But not over—		of excess over—
$188	—$960 . .	$0.00 plus 10%	—$188
$960	—$3,325 . .	$77.20 plus 15%	—$960
$3,325	—$7,783 . .	$431.95 plus 25%	—$3,325
$7,783	—$16,033 . .	$1,546.45 plus 28%	—$7,783
$16,033	—$34,633 . .	$3,856.45 plus 33%	—$16,033
$34,633	—$34,775 . .	$9,994.45 plus 35%	—$34,633
$34,775	. . . .	$10,044.15 plus 39.6%	—$34,775

(b) MARRIED person—

If the amount of wages (after subtracting withholding allowances) is:
Not over $713 . . . . The amount of income tax to withhold is: $0

Over—	But not over—		of excess over—
$713	—$2,258 . .	$0.00 plus 10%	—$713
$2,258	—$6,988 . .	$154.50 plus 15%	—$2,258
$6,988	—$13,371 . .	$864.00 plus 25%	—$6,988
$13,371	—$20,000 . .	$2,459.75 plus 28%	—$13,371
$20,000	—$35,158 . .	$4,315.87 plus 33%	—$20,000
$35,158	—$39,625 . .	$9,318.01 plus 35%	—$35,158
$39,625	. . . .	$10,881.46 plus 39.6%	—$39,625

Publication 15 (2016)

(For Wages Paid in 2016)

TABLE 5—QUARTERLY Payroll Period

(a) SINGLE person (including head of household)—

If the amount of wages (after subtracting withholding allowances) is: The amount of income tax to withhold is:
Not over $563 . . . . $0

Over—	But not over—		of excess over—
$563	—$2,881 . .	$0.00 plus 10%	—$563
$2,881	—$9,975 . .	$231.80 plus 15%	—$2,881
$9,975	—$23,350 . .	$1,295.90 plus 25%	—$9,975
$23,350	—$48,100 . .	$4,639.65 plus 28%	—$23,350
$48,100	—$103,900 . .	$11,569.65 plus 33%	—$48,100
$103,900	—$104,325 . .	$29,983.65 plus 35%	—$103,900
$104,325	. . . .	$30,132.40 plus 39.6%	—$104,325

(b) MARRIED person—

If the amount of wages (after subtracting withholding allowances) is: The amount of income tax to withhold is:
Not over $2,138 . . . . $0

Over—	But not over—		of excess over—
$2,138	—$6,775 . .	$0.00 plus 10%	—$2,138
$6,775	—$20,963 . .	$463.70 plus 15%	—$6,775
$20,963	—$40,113 . .	$2,591.90 plus 25%	—$20,963
$40,113	—$60,000 . .	$7,379.40 plus 28%	—$40,113
$60,000	—$105,475 . .	$12,947.76 plus 33%	—$60,000
$105,475	—$118,875 . .	$27,954.51 plus 35%	—$105,475
$118,875	. . . .	$32,644.51 plus 39.6%	—$118,875

TABLE 6—SEMIANNUAL Payroll Period

(a) SINGLE person (including head of household)—

If the amount of wages (after subtracting withholding allowances) is: The amount of income tax to withhold is:
Not over $1,125 . . . . $0

Over—	But not over—		of excess over—
$1,125	—$5,763 . .	$0.00 plus 10%	—$1,125
$5,763	—$19,950 . .	$463.80 plus 15%	—$5,763
$19,950	—$46,700 . .	$2,591.85 plus 25%	—$19,950
$46,700	—$96,200 . .	$9,279.35 plus 28%	—$46,700
$96,200	—$207,800 . .	$23,139.35 plus 33%	—$96,200
$207,800	—$208,650 . .	$59,967.35 plus 35%	—$207,800
$208,650	. . . .	$60,264.85 plus 39.6%	—$208,650

(b) MARRIED person—

If the amount of wages (after subtracting withholding allowances) is: The amount of income tax to withhold is:
Not over $4,275 . . . . $0

Over—	But not over—		of excess over—
$4,275	—$13,550 . .	$0.00 plus 10%	—$4,275
$13,550	—$41,925 . .	$927.50 plus 15%	—$13,550
$41,925	—$80,225 . .	$5,183.75 plus 25%	—$41,925
$80,225	—$120,000 . .	$14,758.75 plus 28%	—$80,225
$120,000	—$210,950 . .	$25,895.75 plus 33%	—$120,000
$210,950	—$237,750 . .	$55,909.25 plus 35%	—$210,950
$237,750	. . . .	$65,289.25 plus 39.6%	—$237,750

TABLE 7—ANNUAL Payroll Period

(a) SINGLE person (including head of household)—

If the amount of wages (after subtracting withholding allowances) is: The amount of income tax to withhold is:
Not over $2,250 . . . . $0

Over—	But not over—		of excess over—
$2,250	—$11,525 . .	$0.00 plus 10%	—$2,250
$11,525	—$39,900 . .	$927.50 plus 15%	—$11,525
$39,900	—$93,400 . .	$5,183.75 plus 25%	—$39,900
$93,400	—$192,400 . .	$18,558.75 plus 28%	—$93,400
$192,400	—$415,600 . .	$46,278.75 plus 33%	—$192,400
$415,600	—$417,300 . .	$119,934.75 plus 35%	—$415,600
$417,300	. . . .	$120,529.75 plus 39.6%	—$417,300

(b) MARRIED person—

If the amount of wages (after subtracting withholding allowances) is: The amount of income tax to withhold is:
Not over $8,550 . . . . $0

Over—	But not over—		of excess over—
$8,550	—$27,100 . .	$0.00 plus 10%	—$8,550
$27,100	—$83,850 . .	$1,855.00 plus 15%	—$27,100
$83,850	—$160,450 . .	$10,367.50 plus 25%	—$83,850
$160,450	—$240,000 . .	$29,517.50 plus 28%	—$160,450
$240,000	—$421,900 . .	$51,791.50 plus 33%	—$240,000
$421,900	—$475,500 . .	$111,818.50 plus 35%	—$421,900
$475,500	. . . .	$130,578.50 plus 39.6%	—$475,500

TABLE 8—DAILY or MISCELLANEOUS Payroll Period

(a) SINGLE person (including head of household)—

If the amount of wages (after subtracting withholding allowances) divided by the number of days in the payroll period is: The amount of income tax to withhold per day is:
Not over $8.70 . . . . $0

Over—	But not over—		of excess over—
$8.70	—$44.30 . .	$0.00 plus 10%	—$8.70
$44.30	—$153.50 . .	$3.56 plus 15%	—$44.30
$153.50	—$359.20 . .	$19.94 plus 25%	—$153.50
$359.20	—$740.00 . .	$71.37 plus 28%	—$359.20
$740.00	—$1,598.50 . .	$177.99 plus 33%	—$740.00
$1,598.50	—$1,605.00 . .	$461.30 plus 35%	—$1,598.50
$1,605.00	. . . .	$463.58 plus 39.6%	—$1,605.00

(b) MARRIED person—

If the amount of wages (after subtracting withholding allowances) divided by the number of days in the payroll period is: The amount of income tax to withhold per day is:
Not over $32.90 . . . . $0

Over—	But not over—		of excess over—
$32.90	—$104.20 . .	$0.00 plus 10%	—$32.90
$104.20	—$322.50 . .	$7.13 plus 15%	—$104.20
$322.50	—$617.10 . .	$39.88 plus 25%	—$322.50
$617.10	—$923.10 . .	$113.53 plus 28%	—$617.10
$923.10	—$1,622.70 . .	$199.21 plus 33%	—$923.10
$1,622.70	—$1,828.80 . .	$430.08 plus 35%	—$1,622.70
$1,828.80	. . . .	$502.22 plus 39.6%	—$1,828.80

Wage Bracket Method Tables for Income Tax Withholding

SINGLE Persons—WEEKLY Payroll Period

(For Wages Paid through December 31, 2016)

| And the wages are— | | And the number of withholding allowances claimed is— | | | | | | | | | | |
At least	But less than	0	1	2	3	4	5	6	7	8	9	10
		The amount of income tax to be withheld is—										
$0	$55	$0	$0	$0	$0	$0	$0	$0	$0	$0	$0	$0
55	60	1	0	0	0	0	0	0	0	0	0	0
60	65	2	0	0	0	0	0	0	0	0	0	0
65	70	2	0	0	0	0	0	0	0	0	0	0
70	75	3	0	0	0	0	0	0	0	0	0	0
75	80	3	0	0	0	0	0	0	0	0	0	0
80	85	4	0	0	0	0	0	0	0	0	0	0
85	90	4	0	0	0	0	0	0	0	0	0	0
90	95	5	0	0	0	0	0	0	0	0	0	0
95	100	5	0	0	0	0	0	0	0	0	0	0
100	105	6	0	0	0	0	0	0	0	0	0	0
105	110	6	0	0	0	0	0	0	0	0	0	0
110	115	7	0	0	0	0	0	0	0	0	0	0
115	120	7	0	0	0	0	0	0	0	0	0	0
120	125	8	0	0	0	0	0	0	0	0	0	0
125	130	8	1	0	0	0	0	0	0	0	0	0
130	135	9	1	0	0	0	0	0	0	0	0	0
135	140	9	2	0	0	0	0	0	0	0	0	0
140	145	10	2	0	0	0	0	0	0	0	0	0
145	150	10	3	0	0	0	0	0	0	0	0	0
150	155	11	3	0	0	0	0	0	0	0	0	0
155	160	11	4	0	0	0	0	0	0	0	0	0
160	165	12	4	0	0	0	0	0	0	0	0	0
165	170	12	5	0	0	0	0	0	0	0	0	0
170	175	13	5	0	0	0	0	0	0	0	0	0
175	180	13	6	0	0	0	0	0	0	0	0	0
180	185	14	6	0	0	0	0	0	0	0	0	0
185	190	14	7	0	0	0	0	0	0	0	0	0
190	195	15	7	0	0	0	0	0	0	0	0	0
195	200	15	8	0	0	0	0	0	0	0	0	0
200	210	16	8	1	0	0	0	0	0	0	0	0
210	220	17	9	2	0	0	0	0	0	0	0	0
220	230	18	10	3	0	0	0	0	0	0	0	0
230	240	20	11	4	0	0	0	0	0	0	0	0
240	250	21	12	5	0	0	0	0	0	0	0	0
250	260	23	13	6	0	0	0	0	0	0	0	0
260	270	24	14	7	0	0	0	0	0	0	0	0
270	280	26	15	8	0	0	0	0	0	0	0	0
280	290	27	16	9	1	0	0	0	0	0	0	0
290	300	29	17	10	2	0	0	0	0	0	0	0
300	310	30	19	11	3	0	0	0	0	0	0	0
310	320	32	20	12	4	0	0	0	0	0	0	0
320	330	33	22	13	5	0	0	0	0	0	0	0
330	340	35	23	14	6	0	0	0	0	0	0	0
340	350	36	25	15	7	0	0	0	0	0	0	0
350	360	38	26	16	8	0	0	0	0	0	0	0
360	370	39	28	17	9	1	0	0	0	0	0	0
370	380	41	29	18	10	2	0	0	0	0	0	0
380	390	42	31	19	11	3	0	0	0	0	0	0
390	400	44	32	20	12	4	0	0	0	0	0	0
400	410	45	34	22	13	5	0	0	0	0	0	0
410	420	47	35	23	14	6	0	0	0	0	0	0
420	430	48	37	25	15	7	0	0	0	0	0	0
430	440	50	38	26	16	8	0	0	0	0	0	0
440	450	51	40	28	17	9	1	0	0	0	0	0
450	460	53	41	29	18	10	2	0	0	0	0	0
460	470	54	43	31	19	11	3	0	0	0	0	0
470	480	56	44	32	21	12	4	0	0	0	0	0
480	490	57	46	34	22	13	5	0	0	0	0	0
490	500	59	47	35	24	14	6	0	0	0	0	0
500	510	60	49	37	25	15	7	0	0	0	0	0
510	520	62	50	38	27	16	8	0	0	0	0	0
520	530	63	52	40	28	17	9	1	0	0	0	0
530	540	65	53	41	30	18	10	2	0	0	0	0
540	550	66	55	43	31	20	11	3	0	0	0	0
550	560	68	56	44	33	21	12	4	0	0	0	0
560	570	69	58	46	34	23	13	5	0	0	0	0
570	580	71	59	47	36	24	14	6	0	0	0	0
580	590	72	61	49	37	26	15	7	0	0	0	0
590	600	74	62	50	39	27	16	8	1	0	0	0

Wage Bracket Method Tables for Income Tax Withholding

SINGLE Persons—WEEKLY Payroll Period

(For Wages Paid through December 31, 2016)

And the wages are—		And the number of withholding allowances claimed is—										
At least	But less than	0	1	2	3	4	5	6	7	8	9	10
		The amount of income tax to be withheld is—										
$600	$610	$75	$64	$52	$40	$29	$17	$9	$2	$0	$0	$0
610	620	77	65	53	42	30	18	10	3	0	0	0
620	630	78	67	55	43	32	20	11	4	0	0	0
630	640	80	68	56	45	33	21	12	5	0	0	0
640	650	81	70	58	46	35	23	13	6	0	0	0
650	660	83	71	59	48	36	24	14	7	0	0	0
660	670	84	73	61	49	38	26	15	8	0	0	0
670	680	86	74	62	51	39	27	16	9	1	0	0
680	690	87	76	64	52	41	29	17	10	2	0	0
690	700	89	77	65	54	42	30	19	11	3	0	0
700	710	90	79	67	55	44	32	20	12	4	0	0
710	720	92	80	68	57	45	33	22	13	5	0	0
720	730	93	82	70	58	47	35	23	14	6	0	0
730	740	95	83	71	60	48	36	25	15	7	0	0
740	750	96	85	73	61	50	38	26	16	8	0	0
750	760	98	86	74	63	51	39	28	17	9	1	0
760	770	99	88	76	64	53	41	29	18	10	2	0
770	780	102	89	77	66	54	42	31	19	11	3	0
780	790	104	91	79	67	56	44	32	21	12	4	0
790	800	107	92	80	69	57	45	34	22	13	5	0
800	810	109	94	82	70	59	47	35	24	14	6	0
810	820	112	95	83	72	60	48	37	25	15	7	0
820	830	114	97	85	73	62	50	38	27	16	8	0
830	840	117	98	86	75	63	51	40	28	17	9	1
840	850	119	100	88	76	65	53	41	30	18	10	2
850	860	122	102	89	78	66	54	43	31	19	11	3
860	870	124	105	91	79	68	56	44	33	21	12	4
870	880	127	107	92	81	69	57	46	34	22	13	5
880	890	129	110	94	82	71	59	47	36	24	14	6
890	900	132	112	95	84	72	60	49	37	25	15	7
900	910	134	115	97	85	74	62	50	39	27	16	8
910	920	137	117	98	87	75	63	52	40	28	17	9
920	930	139	120	100	88	77	65	53	42	30	18	10
930	940	142	122	103	90	78	66	55	43	31	20	11
940	950	144	125	105	91	80	68	56	45	33	21	12
950	960	147	127	108	93	81	69	58	46	34	23	13
960	970	149	130	110	94	83	71	59	48	36	24	14
970	980	152	132	113	96	84	72	61	49	37	26	15
980	990	154	135	115	97	86	74	62	51	39	27	16
990	1,000	157	137	118	99	87	75	64	52	40	29	17
1,000	1,010	159	140	120	101	89	77	65	54	42	30	19
1,010	1,020	162	142	123	103	90	78	67	55	43	32	20
1,020	1,030	164	145	125	106	92	80	68	57	45	33	22
1,030	1,040	167	147	128	108	93	81	70	58	46	35	23
1,040	1,050	169	150	130	111	95	83	71	60	48	36	25
1,050	1,060	172	152	133	113	96	84	73	61	49	38	26
1,060	1,070	174	155	135	116	98	86	74	63	51	39	28
1,070	1,080	177	157	138	118	99	87	76	64	52	41	29
1,080	1,090	179	160	140	121	101	89	77	66	54	42	31
1,090	1,100	182	162	143	123	104	90	79	67	55	44	32
1,100	1,110	184	165	145	126	106	92	80	69	57	45	34
1,110	1,120	187	167	148	128	109	93	82	70	58	47	35
1,120	1,130	189	170	150	131	111	95	83	72	60	48	37
1,130	1,140	192	172	153	133	114	96	85	73	61	50	38
1,140	1,150	194	175	155	136	116	98	86	75	63	51	40
1,150	1,160	197	177	158	138	119	99	88	76	64	53	41
1,160	1,170	199	180	160	141	121	102	89	78	66	54	43
1,170	1,180	202	182	163	143	124	104	91	79	67	56	44
1,180	1,190	204	185	165	146	126	107	92	81	69	57	46
1,190	1,200	207	187	168	148	129	109	94	82	70	59	47
1,200	1,210	209	190	170	151	131	112	95	84	72	60	49
1,210	1,220	212	192	173	153	134	114	97	85	73	62	50
1,220	1,230	214	195	175	156	136	117	98	87	75	63	52
1,230	1,240	217	197	178	158	139	119	100	88	76	65	53
1,240	1,250	219	200	180	161	141	122	102	90	78	66	55

$1,250 and over   Use Table 1(a) for a **SINGLE person** on page 44. Also see the instructions on page 42.

Wage Bracket Method Tables for Income Tax Withholding

MARRIED Persons—WEEKLY Payroll Period

(For Wages Paid through December 31, 2016)

And the wages are—		And the number of withholding allowances claimed is—										
At least	But less than	0	1	2	3	4	5	6	7	8	9	10
		The amount of income tax to be withheld is—										
$ 0	$170	$0	$0	$0	$0	$0	$0	$0	$0	$0	$0	$0
170	175	1	0	0	0	0	0	0	0	0	0	0
175	180	1	0	0	0	0	0	0	0	0	0	0
180	185	2	0	0	0	0	0	0	0	0	0	0
185	190	2	0	0	0	0	0	0	0	0	0	0
190	195	3	0	0	0	0	0	0	0	0	0	0
195	200	3	0	0	0	0	0	0	0	0	0	0
200	210	4	0	0	0	0	0	0	0	0	0	0
210	220	5	0	0	0	0	0	0	0	0	0	0
220	230	6	0	0	0	0	0	0	0	0	0	0
230	240	7	0	0	0	0	0	0	0	0	0	0
240	250	8	0	0	0	0	0	0	0	0	0	0
250	260	9	1	0	0	0	0	0	0	0	0	0
260	270	10	2	0	0	0	0	0	0	0	0	0
270	280	11	3	0	0	0	0	0	0	0	0	0
280	290	12	4	0	0	0	0	0	0	0	0	0
290	300	13	5	0	0	0	0	0	0	0	0	0
300	310	14	6	0	0	0	0	0	0	0	0	0
310	320	15	7	0	0	0	0	0	0	0	0	0
320	330	16	8	0	0	0	0	0	0	0	0	0
330	340	17	9	1	0	0	0	0	0	0	0	0
340	350	18	10	2	0	0	0	0	0	0	0	0
350	360	19	11	3	0	0	0	0	0	0	0	0
360	370	20	12	4	0	0	0	0	0	0	0	0
370	380	21	13	5	0	0	0	0	0	0	0	0
380	390	22	14	6	0	0	0	0	0	0	0	0
390	400	23	15	7	0	0	0	0	0	0	0	0
400	410	24	16	8	1	0	0	0	0	0	0	0
410	420	25	17	9	2	0	0	0	0	0	0	0
420	430	26	18	10	3	0	0	0	0	0	0	0
430	440	27	19	11	4	0	0	0	0	0	0	0
440	450	28	20	12	5	0	0	0	0	0	0	0
450	460	29	21	13	6	0	0	0	0	0	0	0
460	470	30	22	14	7	0	0	0	0	0	0	0
470	480	31	23	15	8	0	0	0	0	0	0	0
480	490	32	24	16	9	1	0	0	0	0	0	0
490	500	33	25	17	10	2	0	0	0	0	0	0
500	510	34	26	18	11	3	0	0	0	0	0	0
510	520	35	27	19	12	4	0	0	0	0	0	0
520	530	36	28	20	13	5	0	0	0	0	0	0
530	540	38	29	21	14	6	0	0	0	0	0	0
540	550	39	30	22	15	7	0	0	0	0	0	0
550	560	41	31	23	16	8	0	0	0	0	0	0
560	570	42	32	24	17	9	1	0	0	0	0	0
570	580	44	33	25	18	10	2	0	0	0	0	0
580	590	45	34	26	19	11	3	0	0	0	0	0
590	600	47	35	27	20	12	4	0	0	0	0	0
600	610	48	37	28	21	13	5	0	0	0	0	0
610	620	50	38	29	22	14	6	0	0	0	0	0
620	630	51	40	30	23	15	7	0	0	0	0	0
630	640	53	41	31	24	16	8	0	0	0	0	0
640	650	54	43	32	25	17	9	1	0	0	0	0
650	660	56	44	33	26	18	10	2	0	0	0	0
660	670	57	46	34	27	19	11	3	0	0	0	0
670	680	59	47	35	28	20	12	4	0	0	0	0
680	690	60	49	37	29	21	13	5	0	0	0	0
690	700	62	50	38	30	22	14	6	0	0	0	0
700	710	63	52	40	31	23	15	7	0	0	0	0
710	720	65	53	41	32	24	16	8	1	0	0	0
720	730	66	55	43	33	25	17	9	2	0	0	0
730	740	68	56	44	34	26	18	10	3	0	0	0
740	750	69	58	46	35	27	19	11	4	0	0	0
750	760	71	59	47	36	28	20	12	5	0	0	0
760	770	72	61	49	37	29	21	13	6	0	0	0
770	780	74	62	50	39	30	22	14	7	0	0	0
780	790	75	64	52	40	31	23	15	8	0	0	0
790	800	77	65	53	42	32	24	16	9	1	0	0

Wage Bracket Method Tables for Income Tax Withholding

MARRIED Persons—WEEKLY Payroll Period

(For Wages Paid through December 31, 2016)

And the wages are—		And the number of withholding allowances claimed is—										
At least	But less than	0	1	2	3	4	5	6	7	8	9	10
		The amount of income tax to be withheld is—										
$800	$810	$78	$67	$55	$43	$33	$25	$17	$10	$2	$0	$0
810	820	80	68	56	45	34	26	18	11	3	0	0
820	830	81	70	58	46	35	27	19	12	4	0	0
830	840	83	71	59	48	36	28	20	13	5	0	0
840	850	84	73	61	49	38	29	21	14	6	0	0
850	860	86	74	62	51	39	30	22	15	7	0	0
860	870	87	76	64	52	41	31	23	16	8	0	0
870	880	89	77	65	54	42	32	24	17	9	1	0
880	890	90	79	67	55	44	33	25	18	10	2	0
890	900	92	80	68	57	45	34	26	19	11	3	0
900	910	93	82	70	58	47	35	27	20	12	4	0
910	920	95	83	71	60	48	36	28	21	13	5	0
920	930	96	85	73	61	50	38	29	22	14	6	0
930	940	98	86	74	63	51	39	30	23	15	7	0
940	950	99	88	76	64	53	41	31	24	16	8	0
950	960	101	89	77	66	54	42	32	25	17	9	1
960	970	102	91	79	67	56	44	33	26	18	10	2
970	980	104	92	80	69	57	45	34	27	19	11	3
980	990	105	94	82	70	59	47	35	28	20	12	4
990	1,000	107	95	83	72	60	48	37	29	21	13	5
1,000	1,010	108	97	85	73	62	50	38	30	22	14	6
1,010	1,020	110	98	86	75	63	51	40	31	23	15	7
1,020	1,030	111	100	88	76	65	53	41	32	24	16	8
1,030	1,040	113	101	89	78	66	54	43	33	25	17	9
1,040	1,050	114	103	91	79	68	56	44	34	26	18	10
1,050	1,060	116	104	92	81	69	57	46	35	27	19	11
1,060	1,070	117	106	94	82	71	59	47	36	28	20	12
1,070	1,080	119	107	95	84	72	60	49	37	29	21	13
1,080	1,090	120	109	97	85	74	62	50	38	30	22	14
1,090	1,100	122	110	98	87	75	63	52	40	31	23	15
1,100	1,110	123	112	100	88	77	65	53	41	32	24	16
1,110	1,120	125	113	101	90	78	66	55	43	33	25	17
1,120	1,130	126	115	103	91	80	68	56	44	34	26	18
1,130	1,140	128	116	104	93	81	69	58	46	35	27	19
1,140	1,150	129	118	106	94	83	71	59	47	36	28	20
1,150	1,160	131	119	107	96	84	72	61	49	37	29	21
1,160	1,170	132	121	109	97	86	74	62	50	39	30	22
1,170	1,180	134	122	110	99	87	75	64	52	40	31	23
1,180	1,190	135	124	112	100	89	77	65	53	42	32	24
1,190	1,200	137	125	113	102	90	78	67	55	43	33	25
1,200	1,210	138	127	115	103	92	80	68	56	45	34	26
1,210	1,220	140	128	116	105	93	81	70	58	46	35	27
1,220	1,230	141	130	118	106	95	83	71	59	48	36	28
1,230	1,240	143	131	119	108	96	84	73	61	49	38	29
1,240	1,250	144	133	121	109	98	86	74	62	51	39	30
1,250	1,260	146	134	122	111	99	87	76	64	52	41	31
1,260	1,270	147	136	124	112	101	89	77	65	54	42	32
1,270	1,280	149	137	125	114	102	90	79	67	55	44	33
1,280	1,290	150	139	127	115	104	92	80	68	57	45	34
1,290	1,300	152	140	128	117	105	93	82	70	58	47	35
1,300	1,310	153	142	130	118	107	95	83	71	60	48	36
1,310	1,320	155	143	131	120	108	96	85	73	61	50	38
1,320	1,330	156	145	133	121	110	98	86	74	63	51	39
1,330	1,340	158	146	134	123	111	99	88	76	64	53	41
1,340	1,350	159	148	136	124	113	101	89	77	66	54	42
1,350	1,360	161	149	137	126	114	102	91	79	67	56	44
1,360	1,370	162	151	139	127	116	104	92	80	69	57	45
1,370	1,380	164	152	140	129	117	105	94	82	70	59	47
1,380	1,390	165	154	142	130	119	107	95	83	72	60	48
1,390	1,400	167	155	143	132	120	108	97	85	73	62	50
1,400	1,410	168	157	145	133	122	110	98	86	75	63	51
1,410	1,420	170	158	146	135	123	111	100	88	76	65	53
1,420	1,430	171	160	148	136	125	113	101	89	78	66	54
1,430	1,440	173	161	149	138	126	114	103	91	79	68	56
1,440	1,450	174	163	151	139	128	116	104	92	81	69	57
1,450	1,460	176	164	152	141	129	117	106	94	82	71	59
1,460	1,470	177	166	154	142	131	119	107	95	84	72	60
1,470	1,480	179	167	155	144	132	120	109	97	85	74	62
1,480	1,490	180	169	157	145	134	122	110	98	87	75	63

$1,490 and over   Use Table 1(b) for a **MARRIED person** on page 44. Also see the instructions on page 42.

Wage Bracket Method Tables for Income Tax Withholding

SINGLE Persons—**BIWEEKLY** Payroll Period

(For Wages Paid through December 31, 2016)

And the wages are—		And the number of withholding allowances claimed is—										
At least	But less than	0	1	2	3	4	5	6	7	8	9	10
		The amount of income tax to be withheld is—										
$ 0	$105	$0	$0	$0	$0	$0	$0	$0	$0	$0	$0	$0
105	110	2	0	0	0	0	0	0	0	0	0	0
110	115	3	0	0	0	0	0	0	0	0	0	0
115	120	3	0	0	0	0	0	0	0	0	0	0
120	125	4	0	0	0	0	0	0	0	0	0	0
125	130	4	0	0	0	0	0	0	0	0	0	0
130	135	5	0	0	0	0	0	0	0	0	0	0
135	140	5	0	0	0	0	0	0	0	0	0	0
140	145	6	0	0	0	0	0	0	0	0	0	0
145	150	6	0	0	0	0	0	0	0	0	0	0
150	155	7	0	0	0	0	0	0	0	0	0	0
155	160	7	0	0	0	0	0	0	0	0	0	0
160	165	8	0	0	0	0	0	0	0	0	0	0
165	170	8	0	0	0	0	0	0	0	0	0	0
170	175	9	0	0	0	0	0	0	0	0	0	0
175	180	9	0	0	0	0	0	0	0	0	0	0
180	185	10	0	0	0	0	0	0	0	0	0	0
185	190	10	0	0	0	0	0	0	0	0	0	0
190	195	11	0	0	0	0	0	0	0	0	0	0
195	200	11	0	0	0	0	0	0	0	0	0	0
200	205	12	0	0	0	0	0	0	0	0	0	0
205	210	12	0	0	0	0	0	0	0	0	0	0
210	215	13	0	0	0	0	0	0	0	0	0	0
215	220	13	0	0	0	0	0	0	0	0	0	0
220	225	14	0	0	0	0	0	0	0	0	0	0
225	230	14	0	0	0	0	0	0	0	0	0	0
230	235	15	0	0	0	0	0	0	0	0	0	0
235	240	15	0	0	0	0	0	0	0	0	0	0
240	245	16	0	0	0	0	0	0	0	0	0	0
245	250	16	1	0	0	0	0	0	0	0	0	0
250	260	17	1	0	0	0	0	0	0	0	0	0
260	270	18	2	0	0	0	0	0	0	0	0	0
270	280	19	3	0	0	0	0	0	0	0	0	0
280	290	20	4	0	0	0	0	0	0	0	0	0
290	300	21	5	0	0	0	0	0	0	0	0	0
300	310	22	6	0	0	0	0	0	0	0	0	0
310	320	23	7	0	0	0	0	0	0	0	0	0
320	330	24	8	0	0	0	0	0	0	0	0	0
330	340	25	9	0	0	0	0	0	0	0	0	0
340	350	26	10	0	0	0	0	0	0	0	0	0
350	360	27	11	0	0	0	0	0	0	0	0	0
360	370	28	12	0	0	0	0	0	0	0	0	0
370	380	29	13	0	0	0	0	0	0	0	0	0
380	390	30	14	0	0	0	0	0	0	0	0	0
390	400	31	15	0	0	0	0	0	0	0	0	0
400	410	32	16	1	0	0	0	0	0	0	0	0
410	420	33	17	2	0	0	0	0	0	0	0	0
420	430	34	18	3	0	0	0	0	0	0	0	0
430	440	35	19	4	0	0	0	0	0	0	0	0
440	450	36	20	5	0	0	0	0	0	0	0	0
450	460	37	21	6	0	0	0	0	0	0	0	0
460	470	39	22	7	0	0	0	0	0	0	0	0
470	480	40	23	8	0	0	0	0	0	0	0	0
480	490	42	24	9	0	0	0	0	0	0	0	0
490	500	43	25	10	0	0	0	0	0	0	0	0
500	520	46	27	11	0	0	0	0	0	0	0	0
520	540	49	29	13	0	0	0	0	0	0	0	0
540	560	52	31	15	0	0	0	0	0	0	0	0
560	580	55	33	17	2	0	0	0	0	0	0	0
580	600	58	35	19	4	0	0	0	0	0	0	0
600	620	61	37	21	6	0	0	0	0	0	0	0
620	640	64	40	23	8	0	0	0	0	0	0	0
640	660	67	43	25	10	0	0	0	0	0	0	0
660	680	70	46	27	12	0	0	0	0	0	0	0
680	700	73	49	29	14	0	0	0	0	0	0	0
700	720	76	52	31	16	0	0	0	0	0	0	0
720	740	79	55	33	18	2	0	0	0	0	0	0
740	760	82	58	35	20	4	0	0	0	0	0	0
760	780	85	61	38	22	6	0	0	0	0	0	0
780	800	88	64	41	24	8	0	0	0	0	0	0

Wage Bracket Method Tables for Income Tax Withholding

SINGLE Persons—BIWEEKLY Payroll Period

(For Wages Paid through December 31, 2016)

And the wages are—		And the number of withholding allowances claimed is—										
At least	But less than	0	1	2	3	4	5	6	7	8	9	10
		The amount of income tax to be withheld is—										
$800	$820	$91	$67	$44	$26	$10	$0	$0	$0	$0	$0	$0
820	840	94	70	47	28	12	0	0	0	0	0	0
840	860	97	73	50	30	14	0	0	0	0	0	0
860	880	100	76	53	32	16	0	0	0	0	0	0
880	900	103	79	56	34	18	2	0	0	0	0	0
900	920	106	82	59	36	20	4	0	0	0	0	0
920	940	109	85	62	39	22	6	0	0	0	0	0
940	960	112	88	65	42	24	8	0	0	0	0	0
960	980	115	91	68	45	26	10	0	0	0	0	0
980	1,000	118	94	71	48	28	12	0	0	0	0	0
1,000	1,020	121	97	74	51	30	14	0	0	0	0	0
1,020	1,040	124	100	77	54	32	16	1	0	0	0	0
1,040	1,060	127	103	80	57	34	18	3	0	0	0	0
1,060	1,080	130	106	83	60	36	20	5	0	0	0	0
1,080	1,100	133	109	86	63	39	22	7	0	0	0	0
1,100	1,120	136	112	89	66	42	24	9	0	0	0	0
1,120	1,140	139	115	92	69	45	26	11	0	0	0	0
1,140	1,160	142	118	95	72	48	28	13	0	0	0	0
1,160	1,180	145	121	98	75	51	30	15	0	0	0	0
1,180	1,200	148	124	101	78	54	32	17	1	0	0	0
1,200	1,220	151	127	104	81	57	34	19	3	0	0	0
1,220	1,240	154	130	107	84	60	37	21	5	0	0	0
1,240	1,260	157	133	110	87	63	40	23	7	0	0	0
1,260	1,280	160	136	113	90	66	43	25	9	0	0	0
1,280	1,300	163	139	116	93	69	46	27	11	0	0	0
1,300	1,320	166	142	119	96	72	49	29	13	0	0	0
1,320	1,340	169	145	122	99	75	52	31	15	0	0	0
1,340	1,360	172	148	125	102	78	55	33	17	2	0	0
1,360	1,380	175	151	128	105	81	58	35	19	4	0	0
1,380	1,400	178	154	131	108	84	61	37	21	6	0	0
1,400	1,420	181	157	134	111	87	64	40	23	8	0	0
1,420	1,440	184	160	137	114	90	67	43	25	10	0	0
1,440	1,460	187	163	140	117	93	70	46	27	12	0	0
1,460	1,480	190	166	143	120	96	73	49	29	14	0	0
1,480	1,500	193	169	146	123	99	76	52	31	16	0	0
1,500	1,520	196	172	149	126	102	79	55	33	18	2	0
1,520	1,540	199	175	152	129	105	82	58	35	20	4	0
1,540	1,560	203	178	155	132	108	85	61	38	22	6	0
1,560	1,580	208	181	158	135	111	88	64	41	24	8	0
1,580	1,600	213	184	161	138	114	91	67	44	26	10	0
1,600	1,620	218	187	164	141	117	94	70	47	28	12	0
1,620	1,640	223	190	167	144	120	97	73	50	30	14	0
1,640	1,660	228	193	170	147	123	100	76	53	32	16	1
1,660	1,680	233	196	173	150	126	103	79	56	34	18	3
1,680	1,700	238	199	176	153	129	106	82	59	36	20	5
1,700	1,720	243	204	179	156	132	109	85	62	39	22	7
1,720	1,740	248	209	182	159	135	112	88	65	42	24	9
1,740	1,760	253	214	185	162	138	115	91	68	45	26	11
1,760	1,780	258	219	188	165	141	118	94	71	48	28	13
1,780	1,800	263	224	191	168	144	121	97	74	51	30	15
1,800	1,820	268	229	194	171	147	124	100	77	54	32	17
1,820	1,840	273	234	197	174	150	127	103	80	57	34	19
1,840	1,860	278	239	200	177	153	130	106	83	60	36	21
1,860	1,880	283	244	205	180	156	133	109	86	63	39	23
1,880	1,900	288	249	210	183	159	136	112	89	66	42	25
1,900	1,920	293	254	215	186	162	139	115	92	69	45	27
1,920	1,940	298	259	220	189	165	142	118	95	72	48	29
1,940	1,960	303	264	225	192	168	145	121	98	75	51	31
1,960	1,980	308	269	230	195	171	148	124	101	78	54	33
1,980	2,000	313	274	235	198	174	151	127	104	81	57	35
2,000	2,020	318	279	240	201	177	154	130	107	84	60	37
2,020	2,040	323	284	245	206	180	157	133	110	87	63	40
2,040	2,060	328	289	250	211	183	160	136	113	90	66	43
2,060	2,080	333	294	255	216	186	163	139	116	93	69	46
2,080	2,100	338	299	260	221	189	166	142	119	96	72	49

$2,100 and over   Use Table 2(a) for a **SINGLE person** on page 44. Also see the instructions on page 42.

Wage Bracket Method Tables for Income Tax Withholding

MARRIED Persons—**BIWEEKLY** Payroll Period

(For Wages Paid through December 31, 2016)

And the wages are–		And the number of withholding allowances claimed is—										
At least	But less than	0	1	2	3	4	5	6	7	8	9	10
		The amount of income tax to be withheld is—										
$ 0	$340	$0	$0	$0	$0	$0	$0	$0	$0	$0	$0	$0
340	350	2	0	0	0	0	0	0	0	0	0	0
350	360	3	0	0	0	0	0	0	0	0	0	0
360	370	4	0	0	0	0	0	0	0	0	0	0
370	380	5	0	0	0	0	0	0	0	0	0	0
380	390	6	0	0	0	0	0	0	0	0	0	0
390	400	7	0	0	0	0	0	0	0	0	0	0
400	410	8	0	0	0	0	0	0	0	0	0	0
410	420	9	0	0	0	0	0	0	0	0	0	0
420	430	10	0	0	0	0	0	0	0	0	0	0
430	440	11	0	0	0	0	0	0	0	0	0	0
440	450	12	0	0	0	0	0	0	0	0	0	0
450	460	13	0	0	0	0	0	0	0	0	0	0
460	470	14	0	0	0	0	0	0	0	0	0	0
470	480	15	0	0	0	0	0	0	0	0	0	0
480	490	16	0	0	0	0	0	0	0	0	0	0
490	500	17	1	0	0	0	0	0	0	0	0	0
500	520	18	3	0	0	0	0	0	0	0	0	0
520	540	20	5	0	0	0	0	0	0	0	0	0
540	560	22	7	0	0	0	0	0	0	0	0	0
560	580	24	9	0	0	0	0	0	0	0	0	0
580	600	26	11	0	0	0	0	0	0	0	0	0
600	620	28	13	0	0	0	0	0	0	0	0	0
620	640	30	15	0	0	0	0	0	0	0	0	0
640	660	32	17	1	0	0	0	0	0	0	0	0
660	680	34	19	3	0	0	0	0	0	0	0	0
680	700	36	21	5	0	0	0	0	0	0	0	0
700	720	38	23	7	0	0	0	0	0	0	0	0
720	740	40	25	9	0	0	0	0	0	0	0	0
740	760	42	27	11	0	0	0	0	0	0	0	0
760	780	44	29	13	0	0	0	0	0	0	0	0
780	800	46	31	15	0	0	0	0	0	0	0	0
800	820	48	33	17	1	0	0	0	0	0	0	0
820	840	50	35	19	3	0	0	0	0	0	0	0
840	860	52	37	21	5	0	0	0	0	0	0	0
860	880	54	39	23	7	0	0	0	0	0	0	0
880	900	56	41	25	9	0	0	0	0	0	0	0
900	920	58	43	27	11	0	0	0	0	0	0	0
920	940	60	45	29	13	0	0	0	0	0	0	0
940	960	62	47	31	15	0	0	0	0	0	0	0
960	980	64	49	33	17	2	0	0	0	0	0	0
980	1,000	66	51	35	19	4	0	0	0	0	0	0
1,000	1,020	68	53	37	21	6	0	0	0	0	0	0
1,020	1,040	70	55	39	23	8	0	0	0	0	0	0
1,040	1,060	73	57	41	25	10	0	0	0	0	0	0
1,060	1,080	76	59	43	27	12	0	0	0	0	0	0
1,080	1,100	79	61	45	29	14	0	0	0	0	0	0
1,100	1,120	82	63	47	31	16	0	0	0	0	0	0
1,120	1,140	85	65	49	33	18	2	0	0	0	0	0
1,140	1,160	88	67	51	35	20	4	0	0	0	0	0
1,160	1,180	91	69	53	37	22	6	0	0	0	0	0
1,180	1,200	94	71	55	39	24	8	0	0	0	0	0
1,200	1,220	97	73	57	41	26	10	0	0	0	0	0
1,220	1,240	100	76	59	43	28	12	0	0	0	0	0
1,240	1,260	103	79	61	45	30	14	0	0	0	0	0
1,260	1,280	106	82	63	47	32	16	1	0	0	0	0
1,280	1,300	109	85	65	49	34	18	3	0	0	0	0
1,300	1,320	112	88	67	51	36	20	5	0	0	0	0
1,320	1,340	115	91	69	53	38	22	7	0	0	0	0
1,340	1,360	118	94	71	55	40	24	9	0	0	0	0
1,360	1,380	121	97	74	57	42	26	11	0	0	0	0
1,380	1,400	124	100	77	59	44	28	13	0	0	0	0
1,400	1,420	127	103	80	61	46	30	15	0	0	0	0
1,420	1,440	130	106	83	63	48	32	17	1	0	0	0
1,440	1,460	133	109	86	65	50	34	19	3	0	0	0
1,460	1,480	136	112	89	67	52	36	21	5	0	0	0
1,480	1,500	139	115	92	69	54	38	23	7	0	0	0

Wage Bracket Method Tables for Income Tax Withholding

MARRIED Persons—BIWEEKLY Payroll Period

(For Wages Paid through December 31, 2016)

And the wages are—		And the number of withholding allowances claimed is—										
At least	But less than	0	1	2	3	4	5	6	7	8	9	10
		The amount of income tax to be withheld is—										
$1,500	$1,520	$142	$118	$95	$71	$56	$40	$25	$9	$0	$0	$0
1,520	1,540	145	121	98	74	58	42	27	11	0	0	0
1,540	1,560	148	124	101	77	60	44	29	13	0	0	0
1,560	1,580	151	127	104	80	62	46	31	15	0	0	0
1,580	1,600	154	130	107	83	64	48	33	17	2	0	0
1,600	1,620	157	133	110	86	66	50	35	19	4	0	0
1,620	1,640	160	136	113	89	68	52	37	21	6	0	0
1,640	1,660	163	139	116	92	70	54	39	23	8	0	0
1,660	1,680	166	142	119	95	72	56	41	25	10	0	0
1,680	1,700	169	145	122	98	75	58	43	27	12	0	0
1,700	1,720	172	148	125	101	78	60	45	29	14	0	0
1,720	1,740	175	151	128	104	81	62	47	31	16	0	0
1,740	1,760	178	154	131	107	84	64	49	33	18	2	0
1,760	1,780	181	157	134	110	87	66	51	35	20	4	0
1,780	1,800	184	160	137	113	90	68	53	37	22	6	0
1,800	1,820	187	163	140	116	93	70	55	39	24	8	0
1,820	1,840	190	166	143	119	96	73	57	41	26	10	0
1,840	1,860	193	169	146	122	99	76	59	43	28	12	0
1,860	1,880	196	172	149	125	102	79	61	45	30	14	0
1,880	1,900	199	175	152	128	105	82	63	47	32	16	0
1,900	1,920	202	178	155	131	108	85	65	49	34	18	2
1,920	1,940	205	181	158	134	111	88	67	51	36	20	4
1,940	1,960	208	184	161	137	114	91	69	53	38	22	6
1,960	1,980	211	187	164	140	117	94	71	55	40	24	8
1,980	2,000	214	190	167	143	120	97	73	57	42	26	10
2,000	2,020	217	193	170	146	123	100	76	59	44	28	12
2,020	2,040	220	196	173	149	126	103	79	61	46	30	14
2,040	2,060	223	199	176	152	129	106	82	63	48	32	16
2,060	2,080	226	202	179	155	132	109	85	65	50	34	18
2,080	2,100	229	205	182	158	135	112	88	67	52	36	20
2,100	2,120	232	208	185	161	138	115	91	69	54	38	22
2,120	2,140	235	211	188	164	141	118	94	71	56	40	24
2,140	2,160	238	214	191	167	144	121	97	74	58	42	26
2,160	2,180	241	217	194	170	147	124	100	77	60	44	28
2,180	2,200	244	220	197	173	150	127	103	80	62	46	30
2,200	2,220	247	223	200	176	153	130	106	83	64	48	32
2,220	2,240	250	226	203	179	156	133	109	86	66	50	34
2,240	2,260	253	229	206	182	159	136	112	89	68	52	36
2,260	2,280	256	232	209	185	162	139	115	92	70	54	38
2,280	2,300	259	235	212	188	165	142	118	95	72	56	40
2,300	2,320	262	238	215	191	168	145	121	98	75	58	42
2,320	2,340	265	241	218	194	171	148	124	101	78	60	44
2,340	2,360	268	244	221	197	174	151	127	104	81	62	46
2,360	2,380	271	247	224	200	177	154	130	107	84	64	48
2,380	2,400	274	250	227	203	180	157	133	110	87	66	50
2,400	2,420	277	253	230	206	183	160	136	113	90	68	52
2,420	2,440	280	256	233	209	186	163	139	116	93	70	54
2,440	2,460	283	259	236	212	189	166	142	119	96	72	56
2,460	2,480	286	262	239	215	192	169	145	122	99	75	58
2,480	2,500	289	265	242	218	195	172	148	125	102	78	60
2,500	2,520	292	268	245	221	198	175	151	128	105	81	62
2,520	2,540	295	271	248	224	201	178	154	131	108	84	64
2,540	2,560	298	274	251	227	204	181	157	134	111	87	66
2,560	2,580	301	277	254	230	207	184	160	137	114	90	68
2,580	2,600	304	280	257	233	210	187	163	140	117	93	70
2,600	2,620	307	283	260	236	213	190	166	143	120	96	73
2,620	2,640	310	286	263	239	216	193	169	146	123	99	76
2,640	2,660	313	289	266	242	219	196	172	149	126	102	79
2,660	2,680	316	292	269	245	222	199	175	152	129	105	82
2,680	2,700	319	295	272	248	225	202	178	155	132	108	85
2,700	2,720	322	298	275	251	228	205	181	158	135	111	88
2,720	2,740	325	301	278	254	231	208	184	161	138	114	91
2,740	2,760	328	304	281	257	234	211	187	164	141	117	94
2,760	2,780	331	307	284	260	237	214	190	167	144	120	97
2,780	2,800	334	310	287	263	240	217	193	170	147	123	100
2,800	2,820	337	313	290	266	243	220	196	173	150	126	103
2,820	2,840	340	316	293	269	246	223	199	176	153	129	106
2,840	2,860	343	319	296	272	249	226	202	179	156	132	109
2,860	2,880	346	322	299	275	252	229	205	182	159	135	112

$2,880 and over   Use Table 2(b) for a **MARRIED person** on page 44. Also see the instructions on page 42.

Wage Bracket Method Tables for Income Tax Withholding

SINGLE Persons—SEMIMONTHLY Payroll Period

(For Wages Paid through December 31, 2016)

And the wages are—		And the number of withholding allowances claimed is—										
At least	But less than	0	1	2	3	4	5	6	7	8	9	10
		The amount of income tax to be withheld is—										
$ 0	$115	$0	$0	$0	$0	$0	$0	$0	$0	$0	$0	$0
115	120	2	0	0	0	0	0	0	0	0	0	0
120	125	3	0	0	0	0	0	0	0	0	0	0
125	130	3	0	0	0	0	0	0	0	0	0	0
130	135	4	0	0	0	0	0	0	0	0	0	0
135	140	4	0	0	0	0	0	0	0	0	0	0
140	145	5	0	0	0	0	0	0	0	0	0	0
145	150	5	0	0	0	0	0	0	0	0	0	0
150	155	6	0	0	0	0	0	0	0	0	0	0
155	160	6	0	0	0	0	0	0	0	0	0	0
160	165	7	0	0	0	0	0	0	0	0	0	0
165	170	7	0	0	0	0	0	0	0	0	0	0
170	175	8	0	0	0	0	0	0	0	0	0	0
175	180	8	0	0	0	0	0	0	0	0	0	0
180	185	9	0	0	0	0	0	0	0	0	0	0
185	190	9	0	0	0	0	0	0	0	0	0	0
190	195	10	0	0	0	0	0	0	0	0	0	0
195	200	10	0	0	0	0	0	0	0	0	0	0
200	205	11	0	0	0	0	0	0	0	0	0	0
205	210	11	0	0	0	0	0	0	0	0	0	0
210	215	12	0	0	0	0	0	0	0	0	0	0
215	220	12	0	0	0	0	0	0	0	0	0	0
220	225	13	0	0	0	0	0	0	0	0	0	0
225	230	13	0	0	0	0	0	0	0	0	0	0
230	235	14	0	0	0	0	0	0	0	0	0	0
235	240	14	0	0	0	0	0	0	0	0	0	0
240	245	15	0	0	0	0	0	0	0	0	0	0
245	250	15	0	0	0	0	0	0	0	0	0	0
250	260	16	0	0	0	0	0	0	0	0	0	0
260	270	17	0	0	0	0	0	0	0	0	0	0
270	280	18	1	0	0	0	0	0	0	0	0	0
280	290	19	2	0	0	0	0	0	0	0	0	0
290	300	20	3	0	0	0	0	0	0	0	0	0
300	310	21	4	0	0	0	0	0	0	0	0	0
310	320	22	5	0	0	0	0	0	0	0	0	0
320	330	23	6	0	0	0	0	0	0	0	0	0
330	340	24	7	0	0	0	0	0	0	0	0	0
340	350	25	8	0	0	0	0	0	0	0	0	0
350	360	26	9	0	0	0	0	0	0	0	0	0
360	370	27	10	0	0	0	0	0	0	0	0	0
370	380	28	11	0	0	0	0	0	0	0	0	0
380	390	29	12	0	0	0	0	0	0	0	0	0
390	400	30	13	0	0	0	0	0	0	0	0	0
400	410	31	14	0	0	0	0	0	0	0	0	0
410	420	32	15	0	0	0	0	0	0	0	0	0
420	430	33	16	0	0	0	0	0	0	0	0	0
430	440	34	17	0	0	0	0	0	0	0	0	0
440	450	35	18	1	0	0	0	0	0	0	0	0
450	460	36	19	2	0	0	0	0	0	0	0	0
460	470	37	20	3	0	0	0	0	0	0	0	0
470	480	38	21	4	0	0	0	0	0	0	0	0
480	490	39	22	5	0	0	0	0	0	0	0	0
490	500	41	23	6	0	0	0	0	0	0	0	0
500	520	43	25	8	0	0	0	0	0	0	0	0
520	540	46	27	10	0	0	0	0	0	0	0	0
540	560	49	29	12	0	0	0	0	0	0	0	0
560	580	52	31	14	0	0	0	0	0	0	0	0
580	600	55	33	16	0	0	0	0	0	0	0	0
600	620	58	35	18	1	0	0	0	0	0	0	0
620	640	61	37	20	3	0	0	0	0	0	0	0
640	660	64	39	22	5	0	0	0	0	0	0	0
660	680	67	42	24	7	0	0	0	0	0	0	0
680	700	70	45	26	9	0	0	0	0	0	0	0
700	720	73	48	28	11	0	0	0	0	0	0	0
720	740	76	51	30	13	0	0	0	0	0	0	0
740	760	79	54	32	15	0	0	0	0	0	0	0
760	780	82	57	34	17	0	0	0	0	0	0	0
780	800	85	60	36	19	2	0	0	0	0	0	0

Publication 15 (2016)

Wage Bracket Method Tables for Income Tax Withholding

SINGLE Persons—SEMIMONTHLY Payroll Period

(For Wages Paid through December 31, 2016)

And the wages are—		And the number of withholding allowances claimed is—										
At least	But less than	0	1	2	3	4	5	6	7	8	9	10
		The amount of income tax to be withheld is—										
$800	$820	$88	$63	$38	$21	$4	$0	$0	$0	$0	$0	$0
820	840	91	66	40	23	6	0	0	0	0	0	0
840	860	94	69	43	25	8	0	0	0	0	0	0
860	880	97	72	46	27	10	0	0	0	0	0	0
880	900	100	75	49	29	12	0	0	0	0	0	0
900	920	103	78	52	31	14	0	0	0	0	0	0
920	940	106	81	55	33	16	0	0	0	0	0	0
940	960	109	84	58	35	18	1	0	0	0	0	0
960	980	112	87	61	37	20	3	0	0	0	0	0
980	1,000	115	90	64	39	22	5	0	0	0	0	0
1,000	1,020	118	93	67	42	24	7	0	0	0	0	0
1,020	1,040	121	96	70	45	26	9	0	0	0	0	0
1,040	1,060	124	99	73	48	28	11	0	0	0	0	0
1,060	1,080	127	102	76	51	30	13	0	0	0	0	0
1,080	1,100	130	105	79	54	32	15	0	0	0	0	0
1,100	1,120	133	108	82	57	34	17	0	0	0	0	0
1,120	1,140	136	111	85	60	36	19	2	0	0	0	0
1,140	1,160	139	114	88	63	38	21	4	0	0	0	0
1,160	1,180	142	117	91	66	41	23	6	0	0	0	0
1,180	1,200	145	120	94	69	44	25	8	0	0	0	0
1,200	1,220	148	123	97	72	47	27	10	0	0	0	0
1,220	1,240	151	126	100	75	50	29	12	0	0	0	0
1,240	1,260	154	129	103	78	53	31	14	0	0	0	0
1,260	1,280	157	132	106	81	56	33	16	0	0	0	0
1,280	1,300	160	135	109	84	59	35	18	2	0	0	0
1,300	1,320	163	138	112	87	62	37	20	4	0	0	0
1,320	1,340	166	141	115	90	65	40	22	6	0	0	0
1,340	1,360	169	144	118	93	68	43	24	8	0	0	0
1,360	1,380	172	147	121	96	71	46	26	10	0	0	0
1,380	1,400	175	150	124	99	74	49	28	12	0	0	0
1,400	1,420	178	153	127	102	77	52	30	14	0	0	0
1,420	1,440	181	156	130	105	80	55	32	16	0	0	0
1,440	1,460	184	159	133	108	83	58	34	18	1	0	0
1,460	1,480	187	162	136	111	86	61	36	20	3	0	0
1,480	1,500	190	165	139	114	89	64	38	22	5	0	0
1,500	1,520	193	168	142	117	92	67	41	24	7	0	0
1,520	1,540	196	171	145	120	95	70	44	26	9	0	0
1,540	1,560	199	174	148	123	98	73	47	28	11	0	0
1,560	1,580	202	177	151	126	101	76	50	30	13	0	0
1,580	1,600	205	180	154	129	104	79	53	32	15	0	0
1,600	1,620	208	183	157	132	107	82	56	34	17	0	0
1,620	1,640	211	186	160	135	110	85	59	36	19	2	0
1,640	1,660	214	189	163	138	113	88	62	38	21	4	0
1,660	1,680	218	192	166	141	116	91	65	40	23	6	0
1,680	1,700	223	195	169	144	119	94	68	43	25	8	0
1,700	1,720	228	198	172	147	122	97	71	46	27	10	0
1,720	1,740	233	201	175	150	125	100	74	49	29	12	0
1,740	1,760	238	204	178	153	128	103	77	52	31	14	0
1,760	1,780	243	207	181	156	131	106	80	55	33	16	0
1,780	1,800	248	210	184	159	134	109	83	58	35	18	1
1,800	1,820	253	213	187	162	137	112	86	61	37	20	3
1,820	1,840	258	216	190	165	140	115	89	64	39	22	5
1,840	1,860	263	221	193	168	143	118	92	67	42	24	7
1,860	1,880	268	226	196	171	146	121	95	70	45	26	9
1,880	1,900	273	231	199	174	149	124	98	73	48	28	11
1,900	1,920	278	236	202	177	152	127	101	76	51	30	13
1,920	1,940	283	241	205	180	155	130	104	79	54	32	15
1,940	1,960	288	246	208	183	158	133	107	82	57	34	17
1,960	1,980	293	251	211	186	161	136	110	85	60	36	19
1,980	2,000	298	256	214	189	164	139	113	88	63	38	21
2,000	2,020	303	261	218	192	167	142	116	91	66	40	23
2,020	2,040	308	266	223	195	170	145	119	94	69	43	25
2,040	2,060	313	271	228	198	173	148	122	97	72	46	27
2,060	2,080	318	276	233	201	176	151	125	100	75	49	29
2,080	2,100	323	281	238	204	179	154	128	103	78	52	31
2,100	2,120	328	286	243	207	182	157	131	106	81	55	33
2,120	2,140	333	291	248	210	185	160	134	109	84	58	35

$2,140 and over — Use Table 3(a) for a SINGLE person on page 44. Also see the instructions on page 42.

Wage Bracket Method Tables for Income Tax Withholding

MARRIED Persons—SEMIMONTHLY Payroll Period

(For Wages Paid through December 31, 2016)

And the wages are—		And the number of withholding allowances claimed is—										
At least	But less than	0	1	2	3	4	5	6	7	8	9	10
		The amount of income tax to be withheld is—										
$ 0	$360	$0	$0	$0	$0	$0	$0	$0	$0	$0	$0	$0
360	370	1	0	0	0	0	0	0	0	0	0	0
370	380	2	0	0	0	0	0	0	0	0	0	0
380	390	3	0	0	0	0	0	0	0	0	0	0
390	400	4	0	0	0	0	0	0	0	0	0	0
400	410	5	0	0	0	0	0	0	0	0	0	0
410	420	6	0	0	0	0	0	0	0	0	0	0
420	430	7	0	0	0	0	0	0	0	0	0	0
430	440	8	0	0	0	0	0	0	0	0	0	0
440	450	9	0	0	0	0	0	0	0	0	0	0
450	460	10	0	0	0	0	0	0	0	0	0	0
460	470	11	0	0	0	0	0	0	0	0	0	0
470	480	12	0	0	0	0	0	0	0	0	0	0
480	490	13	0	0	0	0	0	0	0	0	0	0
490	500	14	0	0	0	0	0	0	0	0	0	0
500	520	15	0	0	0	0	0	0	0	0	0	0
520	540	17	1	0	0	0	0	0	0	0	0	0
540	560	19	3	0	0	0	0	0	0	0	0	0
560	580	21	5	0	0	0	0	0	0	0	0	0
580	600	23	7	0	0	0	0	0	0	0	0	0
600	620	25	9	0	0	0	0	0	0	0	0	0
620	640	27	11	0	0	0	0	0	0	0	0	0
640	660	29	13	0	0	0	0	0	0	0	0	0
660	680	31	15	0	0	0	0	0	0	0	0	0
680	700	33	17	0	0	0	0	0	0	0	0	0
700	720	35	19	2	0	0	0	0	0	0	0	0
720	740	37	21	4	0	0	0	0	0	0	0	0
740	760	39	23	6	0	0	0	0	0	0	0	0
760	780	41	25	8	0	0	0	0	0	0	0	0
780	800	43	27	10	0	0	0	0	0	0	0	0
800	820	45	29	12	0	0	0	0	0	0	0	0
820	840	47	31	14	0	0	0	0	0	0	0	0
840	860	49	33	16	0	0	0	0	0	0	0	0
860	880	51	35	18	1	0	0	0	0	0	0	0
880	900	53	37	20	3	0	0	0	0	0	0	0
900	920	55	39	22	5	0	0	0	0	0	0	0
920	940	57	41	24	7	0	0	0	0	0	0	0
940	960	59	43	26	9	0	0	0	0	0	0	0
960	980	61	45	28	11	0	0	0	0	0	0	0
980	1,000	63	47	30	13	0	0	0	0	0	0	0
1,000	1,020	65	49	32	15	0	0	0	0	0	0	0
1,020	1,040	67	51	34	17	0	0	0	0	0	0	0
1,040	1,060	69	53	36	19	2	0	0	0	0	0	0
1,060	1,080	71	55	38	21	4	0	0	0	0	0	0
1,080	1,100	73	57	40	23	6	0	0	0	0	0	0
1,100	1,120	75	59	42	25	8	0	0	0	0	0	0
1,120	1,140	77	61	44	27	10	0	0	0	0	0	0
1,140	1,160	80	63	46	29	12	0	0	0	0	0	0
1,160	1,180	83	65	48	31	14	0	0	0	0	0	0
1,180	1,200	86	67	50	33	16	0	0	0	0	0	0
1,200	1,220	89	69	52	35	18	1	0	0	0	0	0
1,220	1,240	92	71	54	37	20	3	0	0	0	0	0
1,240	1,260	95	73	56	39	22	5	0	0	0	0	0
1,260	1,280	98	75	58	41	24	7	0	0	0	0	0
1,280	1,300	101	77	60	43	26	9	0	0	0	0	0
1,300	1,320	104	79	62	45	28	11	0	0	0	0	0
1,320	1,340	107	82	64	47	30	13	0	0	0	0	0
1,340	1,360	110	85	66	49	32	15	0	0	0	0	0
1,360	1,380	113	88	68	51	34	17	0	0	0	0	0
1,380	1,400	116	91	70	53	36	19	2	0	0	0	0
1,400	1,420	119	94	72	55	38	21	4	0	0	0	0
1,420	1,440	122	97	74	57	40	23	6	0	0	0	0
1,440	1,460	125	100	76	59	42	25	8	0	0	0	0
1,460	1,480	128	103	78	61	44	27	10	0	0	0	0
1,480	1,500	131	106	81	63	46	29	12	0	0	0	0
1,500	1,520	134	109	84	65	48	31	14	0	0	0	0
1,520	1,540	137	112	87	67	50	33	16	0	0	0	0
1,540	1,560	140	115	90	69	52	35	18	1	0	0	0
1,560	1,580	143	118	93	71	54	37	20	3	0	0	0
1,580	1,600	146	121	96	73	56	39	22	5	0	0	0

Publication 15 (2016)

Wage Bracket Method Tables for Income Tax Withholding

MARRIED Persons—SEMIMONTHLY Payroll Period

(For Wages Paid through December 31, 2016)

And the wages are—		And the number of withholding allowances claimed is—										
At least	But less than	0	1	2	3	4	5	6	7	8	9	10
		The amount of income tax to be withheld is—										
$1,600	$1,620	$149	$124	$99	$75	$58	$41	$24	$7	$0	$0	$0
1,620	1,640	152	127	102	77	60	43	26	9	0	0	0
1,640	1,660	155	130	105	79	62	45	28	11	0	0	0
1,660	1,680	158	133	108	82	64	47	30	13	0	0	0
1,680	1,700	161	136	111	85	66	49	32	15	0	0	0
1,700	1,720	164	139	114	88	68	51	34	17	0	0	0
1,720	1,740	167	142	117	91	70	53	36	19	2	0	0
1,740	1,760	170	145	120	94	72	55	38	21	4	0	0
1,760	1,780	173	148	123	97	74	57	40	23	6	0	0
1,780	1,800	176	151	126	100	76	59	42	25	8	0	0
1,800	1,820	179	154	129	103	78	61	44	27	10	0	0
1,820	1,840	182	157	132	106	81	63	46	29	12	0	0
1,840	1,860	185	160	135	109	84	65	48	31	14	0	0
1,860	1,880	188	163	138	112	87	67	50	33	16	0	0
1,880	1,900	191	166	141	115	90	69	52	35	18	2	0
1,900	1,920	194	169	144	118	93	71	54	37	20	4	0
1,920	1,940	197	172	147	121	96	73	56	39	22	6	0
1,940	1,960	200	175	150	124	99	75	58	41	24	8	0
1,960	1,980	203	178	153	127	102	77	60	43	26	10	0
1,980	2,000	206	181	156	130	105	80	62	45	28	12	0
2,000	2,020	209	184	159	133	108	83	64	47	30	14	0
2,020	2,040	212	187	162	136	111	86	66	49	32	16	0
2,040	2,060	215	190	165	139	114	89	68	51	34	18	1
2,060	2,080	218	193	168	142	117	92	70	53	36	20	3
2,080	2,100	221	196	171	145	120	95	72	55	38	22	5
2,100	2,120	224	199	174	148	123	98	74	57	40	24	7
2,120	2,140	227	202	177	151	126	101	76	59	42	26	9
2,140	2,160	230	205	180	154	129	104	79	61	44	28	11
2,160	2,180	233	208	183	157	132	107	82	63	46	30	13
2,180	2,200	236	211	186	160	135	110	85	65	48	32	15
2,200	2,220	239	214	189	163	138	113	88	67	50	34	17
2,220	2,240	242	217	192	166	141	116	91	69	52	36	19
2,240	2,260	245	220	195	169	144	119	94	71	54	38	21
2,260	2,280	248	223	198	172	147	122	97	73	56	40	23
2,280	2,300	251	226	201	175	150	125	100	75	58	42	25
2,300	2,320	254	229	204	178	153	128	103	77	60	44	27
2,320	2,340	257	232	207	181	156	131	106	80	62	46	29
2,340	2,360	260	235	210	184	159	134	109	83	64	48	31
2,360	2,380	263	238	213	187	162	137	112	86	66	50	33
2,380	2,400	266	241	216	190	165	140	115	89	68	52	35
2,400	2,420	269	244	219	193	168	143	118	92	70	54	37
2,420	2,440	272	247	222	196	171	146	121	95	72	56	39
2,440	2,460	275	250	225	199	174	149	124	98	74	58	41
2,460	2,480	278	253	228	202	177	152	127	101	76	60	43
2,480	2,500	281	256	231	205	180	155	130	104	79	62	45
2,500	2,520	284	259	234	208	183	158	133	107	82	64	47
2,520	2,540	287	262	237	211	186	161	136	110	85	66	49
2,540	2,560	290	265	240	214	189	164	139	113	88	68	51
2,560	2,580	293	268	243	217	192	167	142	116	91	70	53
2,580	2,600	296	271	246	220	195	170	145	119	94	72	55
2,600	2,620	299	274	249	223	198	173	148	122	97	74	57
2,620	2,640	302	277	252	226	201	176	151	125	100	76	59
2,640	2,660	305	280	255	229	204	179	154	128	103	78	61
2,660	2,680	308	283	258	232	207	182	157	131	106	81	63
2,680	2,700	311	286	261	235	210	185	160	134	109	84	65
2,700	2,720	314	289	264	238	213	188	163	137	112	87	67
2,720	2,740	317	292	267	241	216	191	166	140	115	90	69
2,740	2,760	320	295	270	244	219	194	169	143	118	93	71
2,760	2,780	323	298	273	247	222	197	172	146	121	96	73
2,780	2,800	326	301	276	250	225	200	175	149	124	99	75
2,800	2,820	329	304	279	253	228	203	178	152	127	102	77
2,820	2,840	332	307	282	256	231	206	181	155	130	105	79
2,840	2,860	335	310	285	259	234	209	184	158	133	108	82
2,860	2,880	338	313	288	262	237	212	187	161	136	111	85
2,880	2,900	341	316	291	265	240	215	190	164	139	114	88
2,900	2,920	344	319	294	268	243	218	193	167	142	117	91

$2,920 and over Use Table 3(b) for a **MARRIED person** on page 44. Also see the instructions on page 42.

Wage Bracket Method Tables for Income Tax Withholding

SINGLE Persons—MONTHLY Payroll Period

(For Wages Paid through December 31, 2016)

And the wages are—		And the number of withholding allowances claimed is—										
At least	But less than	0	1	2	3	4	5	6	7	8	9	10
		The amount of income tax to be withheld is—										
$ 0	$220	$0	$0	$0	$0	$0	$0	$0	$0	$0	$0	$0
220	230	4	0	0	0	0	0	0	0	0	0	0
230	240	5	0	0	0	0	0	0	0	0	0	0
240	250	6	0	0	0	0	0	0	0	0	0	0
250	260	7	0	0	0	0	0	0	0	0	0	0
260	270	8	0	0	0	0	0	0	0	0	0	0
270	280	9	0	0	0	0	0	0	0	0	0	0
280	290	10	0	0	0	0	0	0	0	0	0	0
290	300	11	0	0	0	0	0	0	0	0	0	0
300	320	12	0	0	0	0	0	0	0	0	0	0
320	340	14	0	0	0	0	0	0	0	0	0	0
340	360	16	0	0	0	0	0	0	0	0	0	0
360	380	18	0	0	0	0	0	0	0	0	0	0
380	400	20	0	0	0	0	0	0	0	0	0	0
400	420	22	0	0	0	0	0	0	0	0	0	0
420	440	24	0	0	0	0	0	0	0	0	0	0
440	460	26	0	0	0	0	0	0	0	0	0	0
460	480	28	0	0	0	0	0	0	0	0	0	0
480	500	30	0	0	0	0	0	0	0	0	0	0
500	520	32	0	0	0	0	0	0	0	0	0	0
520	540	34	1	0	0	0	0	0	0	0	0	0
540	560	36	3	0	0	0	0	0	0	0	0	0
560	580	38	5	0	0	0	0	0	0	0	0	0
580	600	40	7	0	0	0	0	0	0	0	0	0
600	640	43	10	0	0	0	0	0	0	0	0	0
640	680	47	14	0	0	0	0	0	0	0	0	0
680	720	51	18	0	0	0	0	0	0	0	0	0
720	760	55	22	0	0	0	0	0	0	0	0	0
760	800	59	26	0	0	0	0	0	0	0	0	0
800	840	63	30	0	0	0	0	0	0	0	0	0
840	880	67	34	0	0	0	0	0	0	0	0	0
880	920	71	38	4	0	0	0	0	0	0	0	0
920	960	75	42	8	0	0	0	0	0	0	0	0
960	1,000	80	46	12	0	0	0	0	0	0	0	0
1,000	1,040	86	50	16	0	0	0	0	0	0	0	0
1,040	1,080	92	54	20	0	0	0	0	0	0	0	0
1,080	1,120	98	58	24	0	0	0	0	0	0	0	0
1,120	1,160	104	62	28	0	0	0	0	0	0	0	0
1,160	1,200	110	66	32	0	0	0	0	0	0	0	0
1,200	1,240	116	70	36	2	0	0	0	0	0	0	0
1,240	1,280	122	74	40	6	0	0	0	0	0	0	0
1,280	1,320	128	78	44	10	0	0	0	0	0	0	0
1,320	1,360	134	84	48	14	0	0	0	0	0	0	0
1,360	1,400	140	90	52	18	0	0	0	0	0	0	0
1,400	1,440	146	96	56	22	0	0	0	0	0	0	0
1,440	1,480	152	102	60	26	0	0	0	0	0	0	0
1,480	1,520	158	108	64	30	0	0	0	0	0	0	0
1,520	1,560	164	114	68	34	0	0	0	0	0	0	0
1,560	1,600	170	120	72	38	4	0	0	0	0	0	0
1,600	1,640	176	126	76	42	8	0	0	0	0	0	0
1,640	1,680	182	132	81	46	12	0	0	0	0	0	0
1,680	1,720	188	138	87	50	16	0	0	0	0	0	0
1,720	1,760	194	144	93	54	20	0	0	0	0	0	0
1,760	1,800	200	150	99	58	24	0	0	0	0	0	0
1,800	1,840	206	156	105	62	28	0	0	0	0	0	0
1,840	1,880	212	162	111	66	32	0	0	0	0	0	0
1,880	1,920	218	168	117	70	36	3	0	0	0	0	0
1,920	1,960	224	174	123	74	40	7	0	0	0	0	0
1,960	2,000	230	180	129	78	44	11	0	0	0	0	0
2,000	2,040	236	186	135	84	48	15	0	0	0	0	0
2,040	2,080	242	192	141	90	52	19	0	0	0	0	0
2,080	2,120	248	198	147	96	56	23	0	0	0	0	0
2,120	2,160	254	204	153	102	60	27	0	0	0	0	0
2,160	2,200	260	210	159	108	64	31	0	0	0	0	0
2,200	2,240	266	216	165	114	68	35	1	0	0	0	0
2,240	2,280	272	222	171	120	72	39	5	0	0	0	0
2,280	2,320	278	228	177	126	76	43	9	0	0	0	0
2,320	2,360	284	234	183	132	82	47	13	0	0	0	0
2,360	2,400	290	240	189	138	88	51	17	0	0	0	0

Publication 15 (2016)

Wage Bracket Method Tables for Income Tax Withholding

SINGLE Persons—MONTHLY Payroll Period

(For Wages Paid through December 31, 2016)

And the wages are—		And the number of withholding allowances claimed is—										
At least	But less than	0	1	2	3	4	5	6	7	8	9	10
		The amount of income tax to be withheld is—										
$2,400	$2,440	$296	$246	$195	$144	$94	$55	$21	$0	$0	$0	$0
2,440	2,480	302	252	201	150	100	59	25	0	0	0	0
2,480	2,520	308	258	207	156	106	63	29	0	0	0	0
2,520	2,560	314	264	213	162	112	67	33	0	0	0	0
2,560	2,600	320	270	219	168	118	71	37	3	0	0	0
2,600	2,640	326	276	225	174	124	75	41	7	0	0	0
2,640	2,680	332	282	231	180	130	79	45	11	0	0	0
2,680	2,720	338	288	237	186	136	85	49	15	0	0	0
2,720	2,760	344	294	243	192	142	91	53	19	0	0	0
2,760	2,800	350	300	249	198	148	97	57	23	0	0	0
2,800	2,840	356	306	255	204	154	103	61	27	0	0	0
2,840	2,880	362	312	261	210	160	109	65	31	0	0	0
2,880	2,920	368	318	267	216	166	115	69	35	1	0	0
2,920	2,960	374	324	273	222	172	121	73	39	5	0	0
2,960	3,000	380	330	279	228	178	127	77	43	9	0	0
3,000	3,040	386	336	285	234	184	133	82	47	13	0	0
3,040	3,080	392	342	291	240	190	139	88	51	17	0	0
3,080	3,120	398	348	297	246	196	145	94	55	21	0	0
3,120	3,160	404	354	303	252	202	151	100	59	25	0	0
3,160	3,200	410	360	309	258	208	157	106	63	29	0	0
3,200	3,240	416	366	315	264	214	163	112	67	33	0	0
3,240	3,280	422	372	321	270	220	169	118	71	37	4	0
3,280	3,320	428	378	327	276	226	175	124	75	41	8	0
3,320	3,360	436	384	333	282	232	181	130	80	45	12	0
3,360	3,400	446	390	339	288	238	187	136	86	49	16	0
3,400	3,440	456	396	345	294	244	193	142	92	53	20	0
3,440	3,480	466	402	351	300	250	199	148	98	57	24	0
3,480	3,520	476	408	357	306	256	205	154	104	61	28	0
3,520	3,560	486	414	363	312	262	211	160	110	65	32	0
3,560	3,600	496	420	369	318	268	217	166	116	69	36	2
3,600	3,640	506	426	375	324	274	223	172	122	73	40	6
3,640	3,680	516	432	381	330	280	229	178	128	77	44	10
3,680	3,720	526	441	387	336	286	235	184	134	83	48	14
3,720	3,760	536	451	393	342	292	241	190	140	89	52	18
3,760	3,800	546	461	399	348	298	247	196	146	95	56	22
3,800	3,840	556	471	405	354	304	253	202	152	101	60	26
3,840	3,880	566	481	411	360	310	259	208	158	107	64	30
3,880	3,920	576	491	417	366	316	265	214	164	113	68	34
3,920	3,960	586	501	423	372	322	271	220	170	119	72	38
3,960	4,000	596	511	429	378	328	277	226	176	125	76	42
4,000	4,040	606	521	437	384	334	283	232	182	131	81	46
4,040	4,080	616	531	447	390	340	289	238	188	137	87	50
4,080	4,120	626	541	457	396	346	295	244	194	143	93	54
4,120	4,160	636	551	467	402	352	301	250	200	149	99	58
4,160	4,200	646	561	477	408	358	307	256	206	155	105	62
4,200	4,240	656	571	487	414	364	313	262	212	161	111	66
4,240	4,280	666	581	497	420	370	319	268	218	167	117	70
4,280	4,320	676	591	507	426	376	325	274	224	173	123	74
4,320	4,360	686	601	517	433	382	331	280	230	179	129	78
4,360	4,400	696	611	527	443	388	337	286	236	185	135	84
4,400	4,440	706	621	537	453	394	343	292	242	191	141	90
4,440	4,480	716	631	547	463	400	349	298	248	197	147	96
4,480	4,520	726	641	557	473	406	355	304	254	203	153	102
4,520	4,560	736	651	567	483	412	361	310	260	209	159	108
4,560	4,600	746	661	577	493	418	367	316	266	215	165	114
4,600	4,640	756	671	587	503	424	373	322	272	221	171	120
4,640	4,680	766	681	597	513	430	379	328	278	227	177	126
4,680	4,720	776	691	607	523	438	385	334	284	233	183	132
4,720	4,760	786	701	617	533	448	391	340	290	239	189	138
4,760	4,800	796	711	627	543	458	397	346	296	245	195	144
4,800	4,840	806	721	637	553	468	403	352	302	251	201	150
4,840	4,880	816	731	647	563	478	409	358	308	257	207	156
4,880	4,920	826	741	657	573	488	415	364	314	263	213	162
4,920	4,960	836	751	667	583	498	421	370	320	269	219	168
4,960	5,000	846	761	677	593	508	427	376	326	275	225	174
5,000	5,040	856	771	687	603	518	434	382	332	281	231	180
5,040	5,080	866	781	697	613	528	444	388	338	287	237	186

$5,080 and over   Use Table 4(a) for a **SINGLE person** on page 44. Also see the instructions on page 42.

Wage Bracket Method Tables for Income Tax Withholding

MARRIED Persons—**MONTHLY** Payroll Period

(For Wages Paid through December 31, 2016)

And the wages are—		And the number of withholding allowances claimed is—										
At least	But less than	0	1	2	3	4	5	6	7	8	9	10
		The amount of income tax to be withheld is—										
$ 0	$720	$0	$0	$0	$0	$0	$0	$0	$0	$0	$0	$0
720	760	3	0	0	0	0	0	0	0	0	0	0
760	800	7	0	0	0	0	0	0	0	0	0	0
800	840	11	0	0	0	0	0	0	0	0	0	0
840	880	15	0	0	0	0	0	0	0	0	0	0
880	920	19	0	0	0	0	0	0	0	0	0	0
920	960	23	0	0	0	0	0	0	0	0	0	0
960	1,000	27	0	0	0	0	0	0	0	0	0	0
1,000	1,040	31	0	0	0	0	0	0	0	0	0	0
1,040	1,080	35	1	0	0	0	0	0	0	0	0	0
1,080	1,120	39	5	0	0	0	0	0	0	0	0	0
1,120	1,160	43	9	0	0	0	0	0	0	0	0	0
1,160	1,200	47	13	0	0	0	0	0	0	0	0	0
1,200	1,240	51	17	0	0	0	0	0	0	0	0	0
1,240	1,280	55	21	0	0	0	0	0	0	0	0	0
1,280	1,320	59	25	0	0	0	0	0	0	0	0	0
1,320	1,360	63	29	0	0	0	0	0	0	0	0	0
1,360	1,400	67	33	0	0	0	0	0	0	0	0	0
1,400	1,440	71	37	3	0	0	0	0	0	0	0	0
1,440	1,480	75	41	7	0	0	0	0	0	0	0	0
1,480	1,520	79	45	11	0	0	0	0	0	0	0	0
1,520	1,560	83	49	15	0	0	0	0	0	0	0	0
1,560	1,600	87	53	19	0	0	0	0	0	0	0	0
1,600	1,640	91	57	23	0	0	0	0	0	0	0	0
1,640	1,680	95	61	27	0	0	0	0	0	0	0	0
1,680	1,720	99	65	31	0	0	0	0	0	0	0	0
1,720	1,760	103	69	35	2	0	0	0	0	0	0	0
1,760	1,800	107	73	39	6	0	0	0	0	0	0	0
1,800	1,840	111	77	43	10	0	0	0	0	0	0	0
1,840	1,880	115	81	47	14	0	0	0	0	0	0	0
1,880	1,920	119	85	51	18	0	0	0	0	0	0	0
1,920	1,960	123	89	55	22	0	0	0	0	0	0	0
1,960	2,000	127	93	59	26	0	0	0	0	0	0	0
2,000	2,040	131	97	63	30	0	0	0	0	0	0	0
2,040	2,080	135	101	67	34	0	0	0	0	0	0	0
2,080	2,120	139	105	71	38	4	0	0	0	0	0	0
2,120	2,160	143	109	75	42	8	0	0	0	0	0	0
2,160	2,200	147	113	79	46	12	0	0	0	0	0	0
2,200	2,240	151	117	83	50	16	0	0	0	0	0	0
2,240	2,280	155	121	87	54	20	0	0	0	0	0	0
2,280	2,320	161	125	91	58	24	0	0	0	0	0	0
2,320	2,360	167	129	95	62	28	0	0	0	0	0	0
2,360	2,400	173	133	99	66	32	0	0	0	0	0	0
2,400	2,440	179	137	103	70	36	2	0	0	0	0	0
2,440	2,480	185	141	107	74	40	6	0	0	0	0	0
2,480	2,520	191	145	111	78	44	10	0	0	0	0	0
2,520	2,560	197	149	115	82	48	14	0	0	0	0	0
2,560	2,600	203	153	119	86	52	18	0	0	0	0	0
2,600	2,640	209	158	123	90	56	22	0	0	0	0	0
2,640	2,680	215	164	127	94	60	26	0	0	0	0	0
2,680	2,720	221	170	131	98	64	30	0	0	0	0	0
2,720	2,760	227	176	135	102	68	34	0	0	0	0	0
2,760	2,800	233	182	139	106	72	38	4	0	0	0	0
2,800	2,840	239	188	143	110	76	42	8	0	0	0	0
2,840	2,880	245	194	147	114	80	46	12	0	0	0	0
2,880	2,920	251	200	151	118	84	50	16	0	0	0	0
2,920	2,960	257	206	156	122	88	54	20	0	0	0	0
2,960	3,000	263	212	162	126	92	58	24	0	0	0	0
3,000	3,040	269	218	168	130	96	62	28	0	0	0	0
3,040	3,080	275	224	174	134	100	66	32	0	0	0	0
3,080	3,120	281	230	180	138	104	70	36	3	0	0	0
3,120	3,160	287	236	186	142	108	74	40	7	0	0	0
3,160	3,200	293	242	192	146	112	78	44	11	0	0	0
3,200	3,240	299	248	198	150	116	82	48	15	0	0	0
3,240	3,280	305	254	204	154	120	86	52	19	0	0	0
3,280	3,320	311	260	210	159	124	90	56	23	0	0	0
3,320	3,360	317	266	216	165	128	94	60	27	0	0	0
3,360	3,400	323	272	222	171	132	98	64	31	0	0	0

Publication 15 (2016)

Wage Bracket Method Tables for Income Tax Withholding

MARRIED Persons—**MONTHLY** Payroll Period

(For Wages Paid through December 31, 2016)

And the wages are—		And the number of withholding allowances claimed is—										
At least	But less than	0	1	2	3	4	5	6	7	8	9	10
		The amount of income tax to be withheld is—										
$3,400	$3,440	$329	$278	$228	$177	$136	$102	$68	$35	$1	$0	$0
3,440	3,480	335	284	234	183	140	106	72	39	5	0	0
3,480	3,520	341	290	240	189	144	110	76	43	9	0	0
3,520	3,560	347	296	246	195	148	114	80	47	13	0	0
3,560	3,600	353	302	252	201	152	118	84	51	17	0	0
3,600	3,640	359	308	258	207	156	122	88	55	21	0	0
3,640	3,680	365	314	264	213	162	126	92	59	25	0	0
3,680	3,720	371	320	270	219	168	130	96	63	29	0	0
3,720	3,760	377	326	276	225	174	134	100	67	33	0	0
3,760	3,800	383	332	282	231	180	138	104	71	37	3	0
3,800	3,840	389	338	288	237	186	142	108	75	41	7	0
3,840	3,880	395	344	294	243	192	146	112	79	45	11	0
3,880	3,920	401	350	300	249	198	150	116	83	49	15	0
3,920	3,960	407	356	306	255	204	154	120	87	53	19	0
3,960	4,000	413	362	312	261	210	160	124	91	57	23	0
4,000	4,040	419	368	318	267	216	166	128	95	61	27	0
4,040	4,080	425	374	324	273	222	172	132	99	65	31	0
4,080	4,120	431	380	330	279	228	178	136	103	69	35	1
4,120	4,160	437	386	336	285	234	184	140	107	73	39	5
4,160	4,200	443	392	342	291	240	190	144	111	77	43	9
4,200	4,240	449	398	348	297	246	196	148	115	81	47	13
4,240	4,280	455	404	354	303	252	202	152	119	85	51	17
4,280	4,320	461	410	360	309	258	208	157	123	89	55	21
4,320	4,360	467	416	366	315	264	214	163	127	93	59	25
4,360	4,400	473	422	372	321	270	220	169	131	97	63	29
4,400	4,440	479	428	378	327	276	226	175	135	101	67	33
4,440	4,480	485	434	384	333	282	232	181	139	105	71	37
4,480	4,520	491	440	390	339	288	238	187	143	109	75	41
4,520	4,560	497	446	396	345	294	244	193	147	113	79	45
4,560	4,600	503	452	402	351	300	250	199	151	117	83	49
4,600	4,640	509	458	408	357	306	256	205	155	121	87	53
4,640	4,680	515	464	414	363	312	262	211	160	125	91	57
4,680	4,720	521	470	420	369	318	268	217	166	129	95	61
4,720	4,760	527	476	426	375	324	274	223	172	133	99	65
4,760	4,800	533	482	432	381	330	280	229	178	137	103	69
4,800	4,840	539	488	438	387	336	286	235	184	141	107	73
4,840	4,880	545	494	444	393	342	292	241	190	145	111	77
4,880	4,920	551	500	450	399	348	298	247	196	149	115	81
4,920	4,960	557	506	456	405	354	304	253	202	153	119	85
4,960	5,000	563	512	462	411	360	310	259	208	158	123	89
5,000	5,040	569	518	468	417	366	316	265	214	164	127	93
5,040	5,080	575	524	474	423	372	322	271	220	170	131	97
5,080	5,120	581	530	480	429	378	328	277	226	176	135	101
5,120	5,160	587	536	486	435	384	334	283	232	182	139	105
5,160	5,200	593	542	492	441	390	340	289	238	188	143	109
5,200	5,240	599	548	498	447	396	346	295	244	194	147	113
5,240	5,280	605	554	504	453	402	352	301	250	200	151	117
5,280	5,320	611	560	510	459	408	358	307	256	206	155	121
5,320	5,360	617	566	516	465	414	364	313	262	212	161	125
5,360	5,400	623	572	522	471	420	370	319	268	218	167	129
5,400	5,440	629	578	528	477	426	376	325	274	224	173	133
5,440	5,480	635	584	534	483	432	382	331	280	230	179	137
5,480	5,520	641	590	540	489	438	388	337	286	236	185	141
5,520	5,560	647	596	546	495	444	394	343	292	242	191	145
5,560	5,600	653	602	552	501	450	400	349	298	248	197	149
5,600	5,640	659	608	558	507	456	406	355	304	254	203	153
5,640	5,680	665	614	564	513	462	412	361	310	260	209	159
5,680	5,720	671	620	570	519	468	418	367	316	266	215	165
5,720	5,760	677	626	576	525	474	424	373	322	272	221	171
5,760	5,800	683	632	582	531	480	430	379	328	278	227	177
5,800	5,840	689	638	588	537	486	436	385	334	284	233	183
5,840	5,880	695	644	594	543	492	442	391	340	290	239	189
5,880	5,920	701	650	600	549	498	448	397	346	296	245	195
5,920	5,960	707	656	606	555	504	454	403	352	302	251	201
5,960	6,000	713	662	612	561	510	460	409	358	308	257	207
6,000	6,040	719	668	618	567	516	466	415	364	314	263	213
6,040	6,080	725	674	624	573	522	472	421	370	320	269	219
6,080	6,120	731	680	630	579	528	478	427	376	326	275	225

$6,120 and over Use Table 4(b) for a **MARRIED person** on page 44. Also see the instructions on page 42.

Wage Bracket Method Tables for Income Tax Withholding

SINGLE Persons—DAILY Payroll Period

(For Wages Paid through December 31, 2016)

And the wages are—		And the number of withholding allowances claimed is—										
At least	But less than	0	1	2	3	4	5	6	7	8	9	10
		The amount of income tax to be withheld is—										
$0	$15	$0	$0	$0	$0	$0	$0	$0	$0	$0	$0	$0
15	18	1	0	0	0	0	0	0	0	0	0	0
18	21	1	0	0	0	0	0	0	0	0	0	0
21	24	1	0	0	0	0	0	0	0	0	0	0
24	27	2	0	0	0	0	0	0	0	0	0	0
27	30	2	0	0	0	0	0	0	0	0	0	0
30	33	2	1	0	0	0	0	0	0	0	0	0
33	36	3	1	0	0	0	0	0	0	0	0	0
36	39	3	1	0	0	0	0	0	0	0	0	0
39	42	3	2	0	0	0	0	0	0	0	0	0
42	45	3	2	0	0	0	0	0	0	0	0	0
45	48	4	2	1	0	0	0	0	0	0	0	0
48	51	4	3	1	0	0	0	0	0	0	0	0
51	54	5	3	1	0	0	0	0	0	0	0	0
54	57	5	3	2	0	0	0	0	0	0	0	0
57	60	6	3	2	0	0	0	0	0	0	0	0
60	63	6	4	2	1	0	0	0	0	0	0	0
63	66	7	4	2	1	0	0	0	0	0	0	0
66	69	7	5	3	1	0	0	0	0	0	0	0
69	72	7	5	3	2	0	0	0	0	0	0	0
72	75	8	6	3	2	0	0	0	0	0	0	0
75	78	8	6	4	2	1	0	0	0	0	0	0
78	81	9	7	4	2	1	0	0	0	0	0	0
81	84	9	7	5	3	1	0	0	0	0	0	0
84	87	10	7	5	3	1	0	0	0	0	0	0
87	90	10	8	6	3	2	0	0	0	0	0	0
90	93	11	8	6	4	2	0	0	0	0	0	0
93	96	11	9	6	4	2	1	0	0	0	0	0
96	99	12	9	7	5	3	1	0	0	0	0	0
99	102	12	10	7	5	3	1	0	0	0	0	0
102	105	12	10	8	5	3	2	0	0	0	0	0
105	108	13	11	8	6	4	2	0	0	0	0	0
108	111	13	11	9	6	4	2	1	0	0	0	0
111	114	14	11	9	7	4	3	1	0	0	0	0
114	117	14	12	10	7	5	3	1	0	0	0	0
117	120	15	12	10	8	5	3	2	0	0	0	0
120	123	15	13	10	8	6	3	2	0	0	0	0
123	126	16	13	11	9	6	4	2	1	0	0	0
126	129	16	14	11	9	7	4	3	1	0	0	0
129	132	16	14	12	9	7	5	3	1	0	0	0
132	135	17	15	12	10	8	5	3	2	0	0	0
135	138	17	15	13	10	8	6	3	2	0	0	0
138	141	18	16	13	11	8	6	4	2	1	0	0
141	144	18	16	14	11	9	7	4	2	1	0	0
144	147	19	16	14	12	9	7	5	3	1	0	0
147	150	19	17	15	12	10	8	5	3	2	0	0
150	153	20	17	15	13	10	8	6	3	2	0	0
153	156	20	18	15	13	11	8	6	4	2	1	0
156	159	21	18	16	14	11	9	7	4	2	1	0
159	162	22	19	16	14	12	9	7	5	3	1	0
162	165	22	19	17	14	12	10	7	5	3	1	0
165	168	23	20	17	15	13	10	8	6	3	2	0
168	171	24	20	18	15	13	11	8	6	4	2	1
171	174	25	21	18	16	13	11	9	6	4	2	1
174	177	25	22	19	16	14	12	9	7	5	3	1
177	180	26	22	19	17	14	12	10	7	5	3	1
180	183	27	23	19	17	15	12	10	8	5	3	2
183	186	28	24	20	18	15	13	11	8	6	4	2
186	189	28	25	21	18	16	13	11	9	6	4	2
189	192	29	25	21	18	16	14	11	9	7	4	3
192	195	30	26	22	19	17	14	12	10	7	5	3
195	198	31	27	23	19	17	15	12	10	8	5	3
198	201	31	28	24	20	17	15	13	10	8	6	4
201	204	32	28	24	21	18	16	13	11	9	6	4
204	207	33	29	25	21	18	16	14	11	9	7	4
207	210	34	30	26	22	19	17	14	12	10	7	5
210	213	34	31	27	23	19	17	15	12	10	8	5
213	216	35	31	27	24	20	17	15	13	10	8	6
216	219	36	32	28	24	20	18	16	13	11	9	6
219	222	37	33	29	25	21	18	16	14	11	9	7
222	225	37	34	30	26	22	19	16	14	12	9	7

 Publication 15 (2016)

Wage Bracket Method Tables for Income Tax Withholding

SINGLE Persons—DAILY Payroll Period

(For Wages Paid through December 31, 2016)

And the wages are—		And the number of withholding allowances claimed is—										
At least	But less than	0	1	2	3	4	5	6	7	8	9	10
		The amount of income tax to be withheld is—										
$225	$228	$38	$34	$30	$27	$23	$19	$17	$15	$12	$10	$8
228	231	39	35	31	27	23	20	17	15	13	10	8
231	234	40	36	32	28	24	20	18	15	13	11	8
234	237	40	37	33	29	25	21	18	16	14	11	9
237	240	41	37	33	30	26	22	19	16	14	12	9
240	243	42	38	34	30	26	22	19	17	14	12	10
243	246	43	39	35	31	27	23	20	17	15	13	10
246	249	43	40	36	32	28	24	20	18	15	13	11
249	252	44	40	36	33	29	25	21	18	16	13	11
252	255	45	41	37	33	29	25	22	19	16	14	12
255	258	46	42	38	34	30	26	22	19	17	14	12
258	261	46	43	39	35	31	27	23	19	17	15	12
261	264	47	43	39	36	32	28	24	20	18	15	13
264	267	48	44	40	36	32	28	25	21	18	16	13
267	270	49	45	41	37	33	29	25	21	19	16	14
270	273	49	46	42	38	34	30	26	22	19	17	14
273	276	50	46	42	39	35	31	27	23	19	17	15
276	279	51	47	43	39	35	31	28	24	20	18	15
279	282	52	48	44	40	36	32	28	24	21	18	16
282	285	52	49	45	41	37	33	29	25	21	18	16
285	288	53	49	45	42	38	34	30	26	22	19	17
288	291	54	50	46	42	38	34	31	27	23	19	17
291	294	55	51	47	43	39	35	31	27	24	20	17
294	297	55	52	48	44	40	36	32	28	24	20	18
297	300	56	52	48	45	41	37	33	29	25	21	18
300	303	57	53	49	45	41	37	34	30	26	22	19
303	306	58	54	50	46	42	38	34	30	27	23	19
306	309	58	55	51	47	43	39	35	31	27	23	20
309	312	59	55	51	48	44	40	36	32	28	24	20
312	315	60	56	52	48	44	40	37	33	29	25	21
315	318	61	57	53	49	45	41	37	33	30	26	22
318	321	61	58	54	50	46	42	38	34	30	26	23
321	324	62	58	54	51	47	43	39	35	31	27	23
324	327	63	59	55	51	47	43	40	36	32	28	24
327	330	64	60	56	52	48	44	40	36	33	29	25
330	333	64	61	57	53	49	45	41	37	33	29	26
333	336	65	61	57	54	50	46	42	38	34	30	26
336	339	66	62	58	54	50	46	43	39	35	31	27
339	341	67	63	59	55	51	47	43	39	35	32	28
341	343	67	63	59	55	51	48	44	40	36	32	28
343	345	68	64	60	56	52	48	44	40	36	33	29
345	347	68	64	60	56	52	49	45	41	37	33	29
347	349	69	65	61	57	53	49	45	41	37	34	30
349	351	69	65	61	57	53	50	46	42	38	34	30
351	353	70	66	62	58	54	50	46	42	38	35	31
353	355	70	66	62	58	54	51	47	43	39	35	31
355	357	71	67	63	59	55	51	47	43	39	36	32
357	359	71	67	63	59	55	52	48	44	40	36	32
359	361	72	68	64	60	56	52	48	44	40	37	33
361	363	72	68	64	60	56	53	49	45	41	37	33
363	365	73	69	65	61	57	53	49	45	41	38	34
365	367	73	69	65	61	57	54	50	46	42	38	34
367	369	74	70	66	62	58	54	50	46	42	39	35
369	371	74	70	66	62	58	55	51	47	43	39	35
371	373	75	71	67	63	59	55	51	47	43	40	36
373	375	76	71	67	63	59	56	52	48	44	40	36
375	377	76	72	68	64	60	56	52	48	44	41	37
377	379	77	72	68	64	60	57	53	49	45	41	37
379	381	77	73	69	65	61	57	53	49	45	42	38
381	383	78	73	69	65	61	58	54	50	46	42	38
383	385	78	74	70	66	62	58	54	50	46	43	39
385	387	79	75	70	66	62	59	55	51	47	43	39
387	389	79	75	71	67	63	59	55	51	47	44	40
389	391	80	76	71	67	63	60	56	52	48	44	40
391	393	81	76	72	68	64	60	56	52	48	45	41

$393 and over   Use Table 8(a) for a **SINGLE person** on page 45. Also see the instructions on page 42.

Wage Bracket Method Tables for Income Tax Withholding

MARRIED Persons—**DAILY** Payroll Period

(For Wages Paid through December 31, 2016)

And the wages are—		And the number of withholding allowances claimed is—										
At least	But less than	0	1	2	3	4	5	6	7	8	9	10
		The amount of income tax to be withheld is—										
$0	$39	$0	$0	$0	$0	$0	$0	$0	$0	$0	$0	$0
39	42	1	0	0	0	0	0	0	0	0	0	0
42	45	1	0	0	0	0	0	0	0	0	0	0
45	48	1	0	0	0	0	0	0	0	0	0	0
48	51	2	0	0	0	0	0	0	0	0	0	0
51	54	2	0	0	0	0	0	0	0	0	0	0
54	57	2	1	0	0	0	0	0	0	0	0	0
57	60	3	1	0	0	0	0	0	0	0	0	0
60	63	3	1	0	0	0	0	0	0	0	0	0
63	66	3	2	0	0	0	0	0	0	0	0	0
66	69	3	2	0	0	0	0	0	0	0	0	0
69	72	4	2	1	0	0	0	0	0	0	0	0
72	75	4	3	1	0	0	0	0	0	0	0	0
75	78	4	3	1	0	0	0	0	0	0	0	0
78	81	5	3	2	0	0	0	0	0	0	0	0
81	84	5	3	2	0	0	0	0	0	0	0	0
84	87	5	4	2	1	0	0	0	0	0	0	0
87	90	6	4	2	1	0	0	0	0	0	0	0
90	93	6	4	3	1	0	0	0	0	0	0	0
93	96	6	5	3	1	0	0	0	0	0	0	0
96	99	6	5	3	2	0	0	0	0	0	0	0
99	102	7	5	4	2	1	0	0	0	0	0	0
102	105	7	6	4	2	1	0	0	0	0	0	0
105	108	7	6	4	3	1	0	0	0	0	0	0
108	111	8	6	5	3	1	0	0	0	0	0	0
111	114	8	6	5	3	2	0	0	0	0	0	0
114	117	9	7	5	4	2	0	0	0	0	0	0
117	120	9	7	5	4	2	1	0	0	0	0	0
120	123	10	7	6	4	3	1	0	0	0	0	0
123	126	10	8	6	4	3	1	0	0	0	0	0
126	129	11	8	6	5	3	2	0	0	0	0	0
129	132	11	9	7	5	4	2	0	0	0	0	0
132	135	12	9	7	5	4	2	1	0	0	0	0
135	138	12	10	7	6	4	3	1	0	0	0	0
138	141	12	10	8	6	4	3	1	0	0	0	0
141	144	13	11	8	6	5	3	2	0	0	0	0
144	147	13	11	9	7	5	3	2	0	0	0	0
147	150	14	11	9	7	5	4	2	1	0	0	0
150	153	14	12	10	7	6	4	3	1	0	0	0
153	156	15	12	10	8	6	4	3	1	0	0	0
156	159	15	13	10	8	6	5	3	2	0	0	0
159	162	16	13	11	9	7	5	3	2	0	0	0
162	165	16	14	11	9	7	5	4	2	1	0	0
165	168	16	14	12	9	7	6	4	2	1	0	0
168	171	17	15	12	10	8	6	4	3	1	0	0
171	174	17	15	13	10	8	6	5	3	2	0	0
174	177	18	15	13	11	8	6	5	3	2	0	0
177	180	18	16	14	11	9	7	5	4	2	1	0
180	183	19	16	14	12	9	7	6	4	2	1	0
183	186	19	17	15	12	10	7	6	4	3	1	0
186	189	20	17	15	13	10	8	6	5	3	1	0
189	192	20	18	15	13	11	8	6	5	3	2	0
192	195	21	18	16	14	11	9	7	5	4	2	0
195	198	21	19	16	14	12	9	7	5	4	2	1
198	201	21	19	17	14	12	10	7	6	4	3	1
201	204	22	20	17	15	13	10	8	6	5	3	1
204	207	22	20	18	15	13	11	8	6	5	3	2
207	210	23	20	18	16	13	11	9	7	5	4	2
210	213	23	21	19	16	14	12	9	7	5	4	2
213	216	24	21	19	17	14	12	10	7	6	4	3
216	219	24	22	19	17	15	12	10	8	6	4	3
219	222	25	22	20	18	15	13	11	8	6	5	3
222	225	25	23	20	18	16	13	11	9	7	5	3
225	228	25	23	21	18	16	14	11	9	7	5	4
228	231	26	24	21	19	17	14	12	10	7	6	4
231	234	26	24	22	19	17	15	12	10	8	6	4
234	237	27	24	22	20	17	15	13	10	8	6	5
237	240	27	25	23	20	18	16	13	11	9	7	5
240	243	28	25	23	21	18	16	14	11	9	7	5
243	246	28	26	24	21	19	16	14	12	9	7	6
246	249	29	26	24	22	19	17	15	12	10	8	6

Publication 15 (2016)

Wage Bracket Method Tables for Income Tax Withholding

MARRIED Persons—DAILY Payroll Period

(For Wages Paid through December 31, 2016)

And the wages are—		And the number of withholding allowances claimed is—										
At least	But less than	0	1	2	3	4	5	6	7	8	9	10
		The amount of income tax to be withheld is—										
$249	$252	$29	$27	$24	$22	$20	$17	$15	$13	$10	$8	$6
252	255	30	27	25	23	20	18	16	13	11	8	6
255	258	30	28	25	23	21	18	16	14	11	9	7
258	261	30	28	26	23	21	19	16	14	12	9	7
261	264	31	29	26	24	22	19	17	15	12	10	8
264	267	31	29	27	24	22	20	17	15	13	10	8
267	270	32	29	27	25	22	20	18	15	13	11	8
270	273	32	30	28	25	23	21	18	16	14	11	9
273	276	33	30	28	26	23	21	19	16	14	12	9
276	279	33	31	28	26	24	21	19	17	14	12	10
279	282	34	31	29	27	24	22	20	17	15	13	10
282	285	34	32	29	27	25	22	20	18	15	13	11
285	288	34	32	30	27	25	23	20	18	16	13	11
288	291	35	33	30	28	26	23	21	19	16	14	12
291	294	35	33	31	28	26	24	21	19	17	14	12
294	297	36	33	31	29	26	24	22	19	17	15	12
297	300	36	34	32	29	27	25	22	20	18	15	13
300	303	37	34	32	30	27	25	23	20	18	16	13
303	306	37	35	33	30	28	25	23	21	18	16	14
306	309	38	35	33	31	28	26	24	21	19	17	14
309	312	38	36	33	31	29	26	24	22	19	17	15
312	315	39	36	34	32	29	27	25	22	20	17	15
315	318	39	37	34	32	30	27	25	23	20	18	16
318	321	39	37	35	32	30	28	25	23	21	18	16
321	324	40	38	35	33	31	28	26	24	21	19	17
324	327	41	38	36	33	31	29	26	24	22	19	17
327	330	41	38	36	34	31	29	27	24	22	20	17
330	333	42	39	37	34	32	30	27	25	23	20	18
333	336	43	39	37	35	32	30	28	25	23	21	18
336	339	44	40	37	35	33	30	28	26	23	21	19
339	341	44	40	38	35	33	31	28	26	24	21	19
341	343	45	41	38	36	33	31	29	26	24	22	19
343	345	45	41	38	36	34	31	29	27	24	22	20
345	347	46	42	39	36	34	32	29	27	25	22	20
347	349	46	42	39	37	34	32	30	27	25	23	20
349	351	47	43	39	37	35	32	30	28	25	23	21
351	353	47	43	40	37	35	33	30	28	26	23	21
353	355	48	44	40	38	35	33	31	28	26	24	21
355	357	48	44	40	38	36	33	31	29	26	24	22
357	359	49	45	41	38	36	34	31	29	27	24	22
359	361	49	45	41	38	36	34	31	29	27	24	22
361	363	50	46	42	39	36	34	32	29	27	25	22
363	365	50	46	42	39	37	34	32	30	27	25	23
365	367	51	47	43	39	37	35	32	30	28	25	23
367	369	51	47	43	40	37	35	33	30	28	26	23
369	371	52	48	44	40	38	35	33	31	28	26	24
371	373	52	48	44	41	38	36	33	31	29	26	24
373	375	53	49	45	41	38	36	34	31	29	27	24
375	377	53	49	45	42	39	36	34	32	29	27	25
377	379	54	50	46	42	39	37	34	32	30	27	25
379	381	54	50	46	43	39	37	34	32	30	27	25
381	383	55	51	47	43	39	37	35	32	30	28	25
383	385	55	51	47	44	40	37	35	33	30	28	26
385	387	56	52	48	44	40	38	35	33	31	28	26
387	389	56	52	48	45	41	38	36	33	31	29	26
389	391	57	53	49	45	41	38	36	34	31	29	27
391	393	57	53	49	46	42	39	36	34	32	29	27
393	395	58	54	50	46	42	39	37	34	32	30	27
395	397	58	54	50	47	43	39	37	35	32	30	28
397	399	59	55	51	47	43	40	37	35	33	30	28
399	401	59	55	51	48	44	40	37	35	33	30	28
401	403	60	56	52	48	44	40	38	35	33	31	28
403	405	60	56	52	49	45	41	38	36	33	31	29
405	407	61	57	53	49	45	41	38	36	34	31	29
407	409	61	57	53	50	46	42	39	36	34	32	29

$409 and over — Use Table 8(b) for a **MARRIED person** on page 45. Also see the instructions on page 42.

How To Get Tax Help

If you have questions about a tax issue, need help preparing your tax return, or want to download free publications, forms, or instructions, go to IRS.gov and find resources that can help you right away.

Preparing and filing your tax return. Go to IRS.gov and click on the Filing tab to see your options.

 Getting answers to your tax law questions. On IRS.gov, get answers to your tax questions anytime, anywhere.

- Go to *www.irs.gov/Help-&-Resources* for a variety of tools that will help you with your taxes.

- Additionally, you may be able to access tax law information in your electronic filing software.

Tax forms and publications. You can download or print some of the forms and publications you may need on *www.irs.gov/formspubs*. Otherwise, you can go to *www.irs.gov/orderforms* to place an order and have forms mailed to you. You should receive your order within 10 business days.

Getting a transcript or copy of a return.

- Go to IRS.gov and click on "Get Transcript of Your Tax Records" under "Tools."

- Call the transcript toll-free line at 1-800-908-9946.

- Mail Form 4506-T (transcript request) or Form 4506 (copy of return) to the IRS.

Understanding identity theft issues.

- Go to *www.irs.gov/uac/Identity-Protection* for information and videos.

- If you suspect you are a victim of tax-related identity theft, visit *www.irs.gov/identitytheft* to learn what steps you should take.

Making a tax payment. The IRS uses the latest encryption technology so electronic payments are safe and secure. You can make electronic payments online, by phone, or from a mobile device. Paying electronically is quick, easy, and faster than mailing in a check or money order. Go to *www.irs.gov/payments* to make a payment using any of the following options.

- **Debit or credit card** (approved payment processors online or by phone).

- **Electronic Funds Withdrawal** (available during *e-file*).

- **Electronic Federal Tax Payment System** (best option for businesses; enrollment required).

- **Check or money order**.

IRS2Go provides access to mobile-friendly payment options. Simply download IRS2Go from Google Play, the Apple App Store, or the Amazon Appstore, and make your payments anytime, anywhere.

What if I can't pay now? Click on the "Pay Your Tax Bill" icon on IRS.gov for more information about these additional options.

- Apply for an *online payment agreement* to meet your tax obligation in monthly installments if you cannot pay your taxes in full today. Once you complete the online process, you will receive immediate notification of whether your agreement has been approved.

- An offer in compromise allows you to settle your tax debt for less than the full amount you owe. Use the *Offer in Compromise Pre-Qualifier* to confirm your eligibility.

Understanding an IRS notice or letter. Enter "Understanding your notice" in the search box on IRS.gov to find additional information about your IRS notice or letter.

Visiting the IRS. Locate the nearest Taxpayer Assistance Center using the Office Locator tool on IRS.gov. Enter "office locator" in the search box. Or choose the "Contact Us" option on the IRS2Go app and search Local Offices. Before you visit, use the Locator tool to check hours and services available.

Watching IRS videos. The IRS Video portal *www.irsvideos.gov* contains video and audio presentations for individuals, small businesses, and tax professionals. You'll find video clips of tax topics, archived versions of panel discussions and Webinars, and audio archives of tax practitioner phone forums.

Getting tax information in other languages. For taxpayers whose native language is not English, we have the following resources available.

1. Taxpayers can find information on IRS.gov in the following languages.

   a. *Spanish*.

   b. *Chinese*.

   c. *Vietnamese*.

   d. *Korean*.

   e. *Russian*.

2. The IRS Taxpayer Assistance Centers provide over-the-phone interpreter service in over 170 languages, and the service is available free to taxpayers.

The Taxpayer Advocate Service Is Here To Help You

What is the Taxpayer Advocate Service?

The Taxpayer Advocate Service (TAS) is an **independent** organization within the Internal Revenue Service that helps taxpayers and protects taxpayer rights. Our job is to ensure that every taxpayer is treated fairly and that you know and understand your rights under the _Taxpayer Bill of Rights_.

What Can the Taxpayer Advocate Service Do For You?

We can help you resolve problems that you can't resolve with the IRS. And our service is free. If you qualify for our assistance, you will be assigned to one advocate who will work with you throughout the process and will do everything possible to resolve your issue. TAS can help you if:

- Your problem is causing financial difficulty for you, your family, or your business,
- You face (or your business is facing) an immediate threat of adverse action, or
- You've tried repeatedly to contact the IRS but no one has responded, or the IRS hasn't responded by the date promised.

How Can You Reach Us?

We have offices _in every state, the District of Columbia, and Puerto Rico_. Your local advocate's number is in your local directory and at _www.taxpayeradvocate.irs.gov_. You can also call us at 1-877-777-4778.

How Can You Learn About Your Taxpayer Rights?

The Taxpayer Bill of Rights describes ten basic rights that all taxpayers have when dealing with the IRS. Our Tax Toolkit at _www.taxpayeradvocate.irs.gov_ can help you understand _what these rights mean to you_ and how they apply. These are **your** rights. Know them. Use them.

How Else Does the Taxpayer Advocate Service Help Taxpayers?

TAS works to resolve large-scale problems that affect many taxpayers. If you know of one of these broad issues, please report it to us at _www.irs.gov/sams_.

Index

To help us develop a more useful index, please let us know if you have ideas for index entries. See "Comments and Suggestions" in the "Introduction" for the ways you can reach us.